THE BLENDER COOKBOOK

THE BLENDER COOKBOOK

MARY NORWAK

WARD LOCK LIMITED · LONDON

First published in Great Britain in 1983
by Ward Lock Limited, 82 Gower Street,
London WC1E 6EQ, a Pentos Company.

Text filmset in Linotron Goudy
by Tradespools Limited, Frome, Somerset

Printed and bound in Italy by
Sagdos SpA

British Library Cataloguing in Publication Data

Norwak, Mary
The blender cookbook
1. Blenders (Cookery)
I. title
641.5'89 TX840.B5

ISBN 0-7063-6250-0

Contents

Choosing and Using a Blender	7
Quick Tips	11
Soups	13
Main Courses and Salads	25
Sauces, Dressings and Stuffings	36
Pâtés, Spreads and Dips	46
Puddings, Desserts, Cakes and Icings	55
Preserves and Pickles	71
Sweet Sauces and Drinks	74
Index of Recipes	80

Acknowledgements
Photography (apart from pages 9 and 41) by Martin Brigdale
Home Economist Jacki Baxter
Stylist Gina Carminati

The author and publisher would like to thank the following companies for sponsoring the photographs on pages 17 and 69 (Gales Honey Bureau); page 21 (Philips Small Appliances Ltd) and page 33 (Braun Electric (UK) Ltd).

Photographs on pages 9 and 41 supplied courtesy of Braun Electric (UK) Ltd, Thorn EMI Domestic Appliances Ltd and Moulinex Ltd.

The author and publisher would also like to acknowledge the following companies for kindly loaning equipment for photography:
Casa Pupo Ltd, Ceramique Internationale, The Cocktail Shop, The John Lewis Partnership, David Mellor, Way In-Harrods Ltd.

Notes
It is important to follow *either* the metric *or* the imperial measures when using the recipes in this book. Do not use a combination of measures.

All recipes serve four people, unless otherwise specified.

Choosing and Using a Blender

Types of Blender

A *small blender* may be free-standing or an attachment to a mixer or food processor. It is useful for all blending jobs, plus really fine chopping and grinding. Some free-standing models have special grinder attachments for this work. This type of blender should be run for a few seconds only at a time to avoid overheating, and it should not be used for very stiff mixtures. Food can only be blended in small quantities, so soups and drinks may be laborious and messy to make.

A *large blender* may also be either free-standing or an attachment. It normally has a working capacity of 900ml/ 1½ pints or over. This type of blender can tackle all kinds of blending jobs, and can often be used also for chopping or grinding.

A *wide-based blender* is powerful and not suitable for small quantities of ingredients or for fine chopping; it purées them too soon. However, this type is particularly good for large amounts of drinks or soups, and can also be used for such jobs as rubbing fat into flour.

A *hand blender* has no goblet and may be held in one hand to process food in a bowl. It may be used for making sauces, batters and drinks, whisking eggs, making purées and creaming light pâtés, as well as blending large quantities of soup, or preparing a single portion of baby food.

Although a blender is a useful maid-of-all work, there are one or two jobs better handled by other tools. A blender cannot be used for crushing whole ice cubes (cubes have to be broken into small pieces before adding to liquids in the blender). It cannot be used for processing large quantities of cooked meat, or mincing raw meat, and it will not slice or shave nuts. Although it can be used for making cake batters and for quick creaming of fat, eggs and sugar, it is not suitable for making a complete cake mixture, which is better finished off with a mixer beater. It also cannot be used for mixing light sponge cakes.

Basic Techniques and Maintenance

TECHNIQUES

A blender works by forming a vortex or 'hole' in the mixture. Briefly, the mixture to be blended is pushed up the sides of the goblet and then falls down into the centre and on to the blades. To prevent the blender labouring too hard, start with a small amount of the liquid used in the recipe. Cut fruit, vegetables and meat into small cubes, and break bread or biscuits into small chunks. Remove any fruit stones, or pieces of bones from meat before blending. Use a low speed for chopping and for coarse textures, and start at a low speed increasing to high when larger quantities of food are being blended (over half a goblet full). Work in only small quantities of heavy mixture at a time, and switch quickly 'off' then 'on' to low or high speed to push the food down on to the blades to avoid damaging the machine. Generally, a blender should not run for more than 45–60 seconds at a time. If food gets lodged under the blades, stop the machine and scrape the blades with a rubber or plastic spatula or wooden spoon. Scrape or push the food down from time to time, but do not do this while the motor is running.

Never over-fill the goblet, and always cover it before blending. Hold the lid lightly in place with one hand when starting the motor. The lid should not be taken off during use, unless extra ingredients have to be added while the machine is running, but this is best done by removing the central knob in the lid.

When using a blender recipe, add the ingredients to the goblet in the order given. If you are adapting a normal recipe, try to adapt to blender technique by blending liquids or soft ingredients first, adding ingredients to be chopped or ground after the first blending. See that fats and eggs are at room temperature, or melt the fat before blending. Liquids may be warmed before adding to ease blending, but hot liquids should not be put in the goblet. Be careful not to overblend, since this will spoil the texture of food. Time the blending, using correct speeds, and watch the consistency of food being blended. When chopping such items as nuts, only process a small quantity at a time, or the nuts lower in the goblet will be ground to a fine powder by the time the nuts above are chopped. Follow manufacturers' instructions very carefully if grinding hard substances such as coffee beans, chocolate or nuts, or if preparing raw meat or fish. It is important not to over-process ingredients and to time processing carefully at the correct speed for the job.

A blender motor is dangerously powerful, and children should be kept away from the blender when it is in use. See that nobody puts fingers, hands or implements into the goblet while the motor is running. Do see that it is always firmly attached to the base when running, and standing firmly on a level surface.

Running Speeds

Some blenders have a marked dial, or a series of buttons, either marked 'off', 'low' and 'high', or with a set of numbers. High speed or a high number is for liquid mixtures, while low speed or low numbers are for mixing heavier ingredients, or for chopping.

Quantities

A blender should never be filled more than three-quarters full, and it is wise to divide recipe quantities into small amounts if necessary. Workable blending quantities are:
Liquids: 600ml/1 pint to 900ml/1½ pints, according to size of blender
Pastes and spreads: 100g/4 oz at one time
Bread and biscuit crumbs: 50g/2 oz at one time
Cooked vegetables for purée: 100g/4 oz at one time
Soups: 600ml/1 pint liquid and 225g/8 oz solids
Fruit for purée: 50g/2 oz at one time, without pips or stones
Dried fruit: 50g/2 oz at one time
Batter: 600ml/1 pint

MAINTENANCE

To wash a blender goblet, put into warm soapy water, rinse and dry thoroughly. If food particles are lodged under the blades of a blender, put some warm water and liquid detergent into the blender goblet and run the machine very briefly before rinsing and drying. All plastic parts should be wiped over with hot soapy water and well dried, but not exposed to direct heat such as a cooker or oven. Wash glass parts with hot soapy water, but do not expose them to sudden changes of temperature. Wipe the motor base with a damp cloth and dry well. Do not immerse in water.

A hand blender should be washed by holding the blade part under running water and cleaning the power unit with a damp cloth.

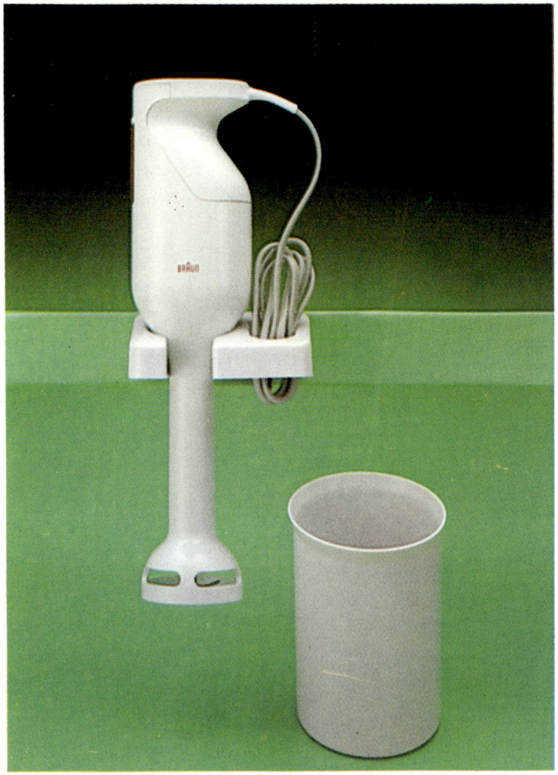

Two types of blender
ABOVE *A hand blender*
RIGHT *A free-standing blender*

Failures and Remedies

Food is chopped too finely

With a blender it is very easy to over-chop so that items such as nuts are ground finely instead of being chopped. Only process small quantities at a time. Work on minimum speed for a very short time.

Food sticks and is not blended

This indicates that there is not enough liquid in a blender goblet, or that a blender is overloaded. Solid ingredients should be added slowly in small quantities so that blending is smooth and even. If the mixture sticks, stop the motor and scrape down the sides, or remove some of the ingredients and process smaller quantities. In a creamed mixture, the ingredients may be too cold.

Cream curdles

This means that cream has been over-mixed. It should be added gradually, and the machine switched off as soon as the cream has been mixed in.

Cheese packs together

Oil is pressed out from some cheeses during blending, and it is a good idea to put a little flour or bread from a recipe into the machine with the cheese during processing so that it absorbs the oil and enables the cheese to grate evenly.

Cheese sauce curdles

This will happen if the raw cheese is blended with the other raw ingredients before cooking, and it will overcook. Grate the cheese separately and add to the cooked sauce.

Icing is too soft

Ingredients in a blender should be at room temperature; if they are too warm, processing will thin the mixture. Leave the icing to firm up before using.

Quick Tips

BISCUITS AND CAKE CRUMBS

Blend broken sweet biscuits on medium speed to make coarse or fine crumbs for flan cases, cheesecake bases, or uncooked biscuit-cakes. Cake crumbs may be blended to use in puddings.

BREADCRUMBS

Crumbs can vary from rough to powder texture, according to their intended use. Fresh bread should be processed in very small amounts. Stale bread will 'crumb' more easily, and bread can be crisped in the oven before blending to make crisp crumbs for coating food.

Break bread into pieces about 2.5cm/1 inch square. Blend a little at a time, stopping the machine to scrape down, and empty out crumbs as they are made.

BUTTER

Blend cream on *high* speed for about 1 minute. Drain off the buttermilk to use for cooking. Put clean cold water into the blender with the cream. Blend for 10 seconds, pour away the water, and squeeze the butter to extract the water. Add salt to taste, and pat the butter into shape.

CHEESE

Cut cheese into 2.5cm/1 inch cubes and feed gradually into the blender. Very hard cheese such as Parmesan should be cut into smaller pieces. As soon as the cheese becomes sticky, switch off, empty out the cheese, and process another quantity. About 50g/2oz cheese should be processed in each batch. High speed for 6 seconds should be enough to grate most cheeses.

CHILDREN'S FOOD

Food suitable for young children can be easily blended. This means that meat, fish, poultry and vegetables from the ordinary family meal can be utilized; fruit and custard or milk puddings or cereal can be blended for a sweet course.

Dried milk for babies can be smoothly prepared in a blender which has been washed, rinsed and scalded before use. Powdered cereals can also be added to the milk in the blender. Flavoured milk drinks, or combinations of milk and eggs, or milk and fruit, will be popular with older children.

CHOCOLATE

Block chocolate should be broken up in small pieces and processed in a blender at low speed to the required fineness. Not more than 75g/3oz should be chopped or grated at one time.

HEALTH FOODS

A blender can be used to retain the complete goodness of fruit and vegetables for soups and drinks. Yoghurt can be blended into drinks, and wheatgerm added for extra nourishment. Those who wish to avoid flour or fats will find that sauces and soups can be easily made without thickening.

HERBS

Chop herbs in a blender by dropping sprigs of fresh herbs on to the cutters as they rotate. A little liquid aids easy blending.

PRALINE

Home-made praline is very useful for flavouring and decorating soufflés, creams and ices. Put together 75g/3oz caster sugar and 75g/3oz whole unblanched almonds in a thick saucepan, and set over low heat. Do not stir until the sugar has melted and is turning in colour. Stir frequently until a rich caramel colour, with the almonds well toasted. Turn on to an oiled tin. When hard, break into pieces and blend on *low* speed until powdery. Keep in an airtight tin.

If preferred, nut brittle may be bought and processed in the same way.

PURÉES

Soft raw vegetables and fruit such as tomatoes and strawberries, or cooked fruit or vegetables, need no extra liquid to become purée. They may be blended on *high* speed and sieved if necessary. The goblet should only be half-full, and fruit need not be peeled before converting it into purée.

SUGAR

Granulated sugar may be refined by blending at maximum speed for 30 seconds to produce caster sugar. Do not fill the blender goblet more than a quarter full. Caster sugar may be reduced to a powder to use as icing sugar, but will be slightly gritty and greyish in colour. Coloured sugar can be made for cakes and puddings if a few drops of food colouring are added during processing. The sugar should be stirred with a spatula once during blending to distribute colour.

SOUPS

TOMATO SOUP

1 small onion
1 bacon rasher, without rinds
25g/1 oz butter **or** bacon fat
450g/1 lb ripe tomatoes (see **Note**)
1 medium potato
300ml/½ pint water
1 × 5ml spoon/1 teaspoon salt
1 × 2.5ml spoon/½ teaspoon sugar
1 × 2.5ml spoon/½ teaspoon paprika
1 × 2.5ml spoon/½ teaspoon celery salt
½ × 2.5 spoon/¼ teaspoon Cayenne pepper
150ml/¼ pint milk

GARNISH
whipped cream
chopped parsley

Cut the onion into pieces with the bacon, then soften in the butter or bacon fat until the onion is golden-brown. Skin the tomatoes and remove the pips. Peel and slice the potato. Add with the tomatoes and water to the onion and bacon, cover and simmer for 30 minutes. Blend for 1 minute with the seasonings, then add the milk, and blend for 10 seconds. Re-heat the soup gently, and serve with a garnish of whipped cream and chopped parsley.

Note If fresh tomatoes are out of season, canned tomatoes can be used. Substitute 450g/1 lb canned tomatoes, including the liquid, but sieve the soup after blending to get rid of the pips.

CELERY SOUP

10 sticks celery
1 medium onion
900ml/1½ pints chicken stock
1 × 5ml spoon/1 teaspoon salt

Cut the celery into 2.5cm/1 inch pieces. Cut the onion into pieces. Blend with the celery and stock in small quantities until the vegetables are coarsely chopped. Put into a saucepan with the salt, bring to the boil, then simmer for 10 minutes. Blend until smooth. Re-heat and serve hot with cubes of fried bread.

Variation

If a cream soup is preferred, use 300ml/½ pint creamy milk instead of part of the stock, and add it at the second blending stage.

CHESTNUT SOUP

1 medium onion
1 carrot
2 leeks
3 sticks celery
50g/2 oz butter
1.2 litres/2 pints milk
salt and pepper
36 chestnuts

Cut the onion, carrot, leeks and celery in pieces and blend in small quantities until finely chopped. Melt the butter and cook the vegetables gently until soft and golden. Add the milk and seasoning, and simmer for 1 hour.

Meanwhile, shell and peel the chestnuts, then simmer them in half the liquid for 1½ hours. Reserve six nuts to use as a garnish, and blend the remaining chestnuts, the cooking liquid and the vegetables. Re-heat for 10 minutes.

Mushroom Soup

225g/8 oz mushrooms
1.2 litres/2 pints water
1 small onion
50g/2 oz butter
40g/1½ oz plain flour
150ml/¼ pint milk
salt
a pinch of nutmeg
150ml/¼ pint single cream

GARNISH
chopped parsley

Cut the mushrooms into pieces and blend with half the water for 5 seconds. Blend the onion until chopped. Melt the butter in a pan, and cook the onion until glossy, then stir in the flour, and cook until light yellow in colour. Add the mushroom mixture with the remaining water and the milk, and simmer for 10 minutes. Season with salt and a pinch of nutmeg. Just before serving, add the cream, and garnish with chopped parsley.

Country Carrot Soup

675g/1½ lb carrots
450g/1 lb potatoes
225g/8 oz onions
1.2 litres/2 pints chicken stock
75g/3 oz butter
salt and pepper
1 bay leaf
a sprig of thyme
a sprig of parsley

GARNISH
chopped parsley

Blend the carrots until chopped. Quarter the potatoes and onions, and blend until chopped, adding a little stock if necessary. Melt the butter in a saucepan and cook the onions gently for 5 minutes, stirring well. Add the carrots and potatoes, and continue cooking for 10 minutes, stirring often. Add the stock, salt, pepper, bay leaf, thyme and parsley sprig. Bring to the boil, then cover and simmer for 25 minutes until the vegetables are soft. Remove the bay leaf, thyme and parsley. Strain the liquid into a clean pan. Blend the vegetables until smooth and creamy, adding a little cooking liquid if necessary. Add to the liquid in the pan and re-heat gently. Sprinkle the chopped parsley over the soup just before serving. If liked, serve with small cubes of toasted or fried bread.

Cream of Onion Soup

2 rashers streaky bacon, without rinds
225g/8 oz onions
25g/1 oz butter
15g/½ oz flour
900ml/1½ pints milk
salt and pepper
40g/1½ oz cheese

GARNISH
chopped parsley

Cut the bacon in pieces and blend until coarsely chopped. Fry gently to extract the fat. Cut the onions in pieces and blend until finely chopped. Add to the bacon with the butter, and cook slowly until the onions are soft but not coloured. Sprinkle in the flour, mix well and gradually add the milk and seasoning. Bring to the boil and simmer for 10 minutes. Blend until smooth, then reheat gently. Blend the cheese until chopped and put it into a tureen. Pour on the soup, and garnish with a little chopped parsley.

Florentine Soup

900g/2 lb fresh spinach
100g/4 oz onions
50g/2 oz butter
900ml/1½ pints chicken stock
salt and pepper
a pinch of ground nutmeg
4 × 15ml spoons/4 tablespoons single cream
50g/2 oz Cheddar cheese

Put the spinach leaves into a large saucepan and just cover with boiling water. Bring to the boil quickly and drain thoroughly. Cool completely under running water. Blend the onions until finely chopped. Melt the butter in a pan and stir the onions over low heat for 5 minutes until soft and golden. Drain the spinach thoroughly and add to the pan. Stir well to coat with butter, cover and simmer for 10 minutes. Cool slightly and blend until smooth. Return to the pan with the stock, salt, pepper and nutmeg. Bring to the boil, cover and simmer for 15 minutes. Just before serving, stir in the cream. Chop the cheese in the blender and sprinkle generously over each portion of soup.

Leek and Potato Soup

450g/1 lb potatoes
450g/1 lb leeks
50g/2 oz butter
750ml/$1\frac{1}{4}$ pints chicken stock
300ml/$\frac{1}{2}$ pint milk
salt and pepper

GARNISH
chopped chives

Cut the potatoes into pieces with the leek. Melt the butter in a pan, add the vegetables and simmer for 5 minutes. Add the stock, cover and simmer for 20 minutes, then blend for 10 seconds. Add the milk and blend for 5 seconds. Re-heat gently, seasoning with salt and pepper, and garnish with chopped chives.

Variation

Chill the soup and add a little thin cream. Serve chilled. This soup is called Vichyssoise.

Chilled Avocado Soup

2 medium avocado pears
1 small onion
2 cloves garlic
450ml/$\frac{3}{4}$ pint milk
150ml/$\frac{1}{4}$ pint natural yoghurt

Halve the avocado pears and scoop out the flesh. Cut the onion into pieces. Add with the garlic, milk and yoghurt to the avocado pears, and blend until completely smooth.

Note Use soft ripe avocados, and make the soup about 1 hour before serving so that there is time to chill it without taking away the delicate flavour.

Chilled Beetroot Soup

450g/1 lb cooked beetroot
900ml/$1\frac{1}{2}$ pints water
2 small lemons
3 size 3–4 eggs
1 × 5ml spoon/1 teaspoon salt
1 × 15ml spoon/1 tablespoon clear honey

Peel the beetroot and cut into pieces. Blend with the water until finely chopped. Put into a saucepan and bring to the boil. Meanwhile, peel the lemons and remove the pips. Cut the flesh into pieces and blend until smooth. Add to the beetroot, and simmer for 15 minutes. Remove from the heat and cool for 10 minutes.

In a bowl, mix the eggs, salt and honey, and gradually pour in the beetroot mixture. Stir well and serve cold.

If liked, the soup can be blended a second time when the eggs have been added, until completely smooth.

Chilled Cucumber Soup

2 large cucumbers
600ml/1 pint natural yoghurt
1 × 5ml spoon/1 teaspoon salt
a pinch of nutmeg

GARNISH
2 × 5ml spoons/2 teaspoons chopped dill

Trim the ends from the cucumbers, but do not peel them. Cut a few very thin slices to use as a garnish. Cut the cucumbers into pieces and blend until smooth with the yoghurt, salt, nutmeg and half the dill. Chill. Serve garnished with chopped dill and the reserved cucumber slices.

Chilled Beetroot Soup

GALE'S
PURE COUNTRY
HONEY

Split Pea Soup

100g/4 oz split peas
1 large onion
1 medium carrot
1 medium turnip
1 bacon rasher, without rinds
25g/1 oz butter
1 × 5ml spoon/1 teaspoon sugar
900ml/1½ pints stock
300ml/½ pint milk
salt and pepper

GARNISH
croûtons of fried bread

Blend the split peas for 1 minute. Cut the vegetables and bacon into small pieces. Melt the butter in a saucepan and cook the onion and bacon until golden-brown. Add the carrot and turnip and cook for 2 minutes, stirring well. Add the split peas, sugar and stock, and simmer for 45 minutes. Blend for 1 minute with the milk, then re-heat, seasoning with salt and pepper to taste. Garnish with croûtons of fried bread.

Fresh Pea Soup

1 small onion
50g/2 oz butter
450g/1 lb shelled green peas (see **Note**)
a pinch of mace
a sprig of parsley
1 × 2.5ml spoon/½ teaspoon salt
1 × 5ml spoon/1 teaspoon sugar
450ml/¾ pint water
300ml/½ pint creamy milk
pepper

GARNISH
chopped mint
fried croûtons **or** crumbled crisp bacon

Blend the onion until coarsely chopped. Melt the butter in a pan and cook the onion until soft. Add the peas, mace, parsley, salt, sugar and water, and simmer for 20 minutes. Blend for 1 minute. Add the milk, and blend for 10 seconds. Re-heat gently, and season with pepper and more salt to taste. Garnish with a little chopped mint and with fried croûtons or crumbled crisp bacon.

Note If fresh peas are not available, use the equivalent weight of frozen peas, and let them thaw slightly before using.

Watercress Soup

450g/1 lb potatoes
900ml/1½ pints chicken stock
1 bunch watercress
15g/½ oz cornflour
300ml/½ pint milk
salt and pepper

GARNISH
watercress leaves

Cut the potatoes into pieces and cook in the chicken stock for 25 minutes, then blend with the watercress until smooth. Mix the cornflour with a little milk or water, and add with the rest of the milk to the vegetables. Blend for 10 seconds. Re-heat the soup, seasoning to taste, and garnish with a few watercress leaves.

Beef Broth

225g/8 oz shin of beef
1.2 litres/2 pints water
salt and pepper
1 medium carrot
1 medium onion
1 small turnip
1 stick celery
25g/1 oz dripping

GARNISH
1 × 15ml spoon/1 tablespoon chopped parsley

Cut the beef into small pieces and put into the water with the salt and pepper. Cover and simmer for 1 hour. Blend the vegetables until coarsely chopped, then fry until soft and golden in the dripping. Add to the stock, and simmer for 1 hour. Blend until smooth and season to taste. Re-heat and garnish with chopped parsley.

Thick Oxtail Soup

25g/1 oz dripping
450g/1 lb oxtail
1 large onion
1 medium carrot
1 small turnip
1 small leek
15g/½ oz plain flour
2 × 5ml spoons/2 teaspoons concentrated tomato purée
1 bay leaf
a sprig of parsley
a sprig of thyme
salt and pepper
1.8 litres/3 pints boiling water
15g/½ oz cornflour
3 × 15ml spoons/3 tablespoons dry sherry

Heat the dripping in a pan, cut the oxtail into pieces and brown lightly. Remove the oxtail pieces and put to one side. Blend the onion with the other vegetables until coarsely chopped. Brown lightly in the fat. Replace the meat and stir in the flour and tomato purée. Add the herbs, seasoning and water, and mix well. Cover and simmer for 4 hours. Leave until cold, then skim. Remove the meat from the bones and blend with the vegetables, stock and cornflour until almost smooth. Return to the pan and simmer for 10 minutes. Stir in the sherry and serve at once.

One-pot Soup

1 lemon
1.6kg/3½ lb chicken
2 medium carrots
3 leeks
4 sticks celery
2 medium onions
15g/½ oz butter
1 bay leaf
a sprig of parsley
a sprig of thyme
900ml/1½ pints chicken stock
375ml/13 fl oz dry white wine
salt and pepper
1 × 15ml spoon/1 tablespoon fresh parsley
25g/1 oz stale bread
1 × 15ml spoon/1 tablespoon oil
15g/½ oz butter

Cut the lemon in half and rub the cut sides all over the chicken. Cut the carrots, leeks, celery and onions into pieces and blend until finely chopped. Melt the butter in a pan and stir the vegetables over low heat for 5 minutes.

Put the chicken into a large pan with the vegetables, herbs and stock. Bring to the boil, then add the wine and seasoning. Cover, bring to the boil, and simmer for 1½ hours or until the chicken is tender. Discard the herbs.

Cut the chicken from the bones and blend until coarsely chopped. Put into the pan with the vegetables and liquid and simmer for 5 minutes, adjusting the seasoning. Chop the parsley and add to the soup.

Break the bread into pieces and make into crumbs in the blender. Fry the crumbs in hot oil and butter until golden. Serve each bowl of soup with a sprinkling of golden crumbs.

Chicken Soup with Parsley Balls

1.2 litres/2 pints chicken stock
225g/8 oz cooked chicken
15g/½ oz plain flour
salt and pepper

PARSLEY BALLS
2 eggs
1 × 15ml spoon/1 tablespoon fresh parsley
50g/2 oz softened butter
75g/3 oz self-raising flour
salt and pepper

Put the chicken stock into a large pan. Cut the chicken into pieces and blend with the flour, salt and pepper, and with 150ml/¼ pint of the chicken stock until the chicken is coarsely chopped. Add to the stock in the pan, bring to the boil and simmer for 10 minutes.

To make the parsley balls, blend together the eggs, parsley and butter until the parsley is finely chopped. Add the flour and seasoning, and blend to make a soft dough. Drop teaspoonfuls of the mixture into the simmering soup and cook for 5 minutes. Serve a few parsley balls in each bowl of soup.

Creamed Fish Soup (page 24), Watercress Soup (page 19) and *One-pot Soup*

PHILIPS
0 1

Chicken and Pea Soup

1 small onion
1 small lettuce
675g/1½ lb shelled peas (see **Note**)
50g/2 oz butter
100g/4 oz fresh spinach
a sprig of parsley
salt and pepper
1 × 5ml spoon/1 teaspoon sugar
900ml/1½ pints chicken stock
50g/2 oz cooked chicken
2 egg yolks
300ml/½ pint single cream

Cut the onion into pieces and blend until coarsely chopped. Shred the lettuce. Reserve 100g/4 oz peas and put the rest into a pan with the butter, onion, lettuce, spinach, parsley, salt, pepper, sugar and stock. Bring to the boil, cover and simmer for 20 minutes. Blend the soup until smooth, then simmer for 5 minutes. Blend the chicken until finely chopped and add to the soup with the remaining peas. Simmer for 5 minutes. Blend the egg yolks and cream until well mixed. Add 4 × 15ml spoons/4 tablespoons hot soup, and blend until well mixed. Stir into the hot soup and re-heat gently, but do not boil.

Note Frozen peas may be used, and should be just thawed.

Bacon Soup with Sausage Dumplings

350g/12 oz collar bacon joint
1.2 litres/2 pints water
1 bay leaf
4 medium carrots
2 medium onions
1 medium parsnip
½ small white cabbage
salt and pepper
1 × 15ml spoon/1 tablespoon tomato chutney

DUMPLINGS
100g/4 oz self-raising flour
25g/1 oz shredded suet
100g/4 oz pork sausage-meat
1 × 15ml spoon/1 tablespoon fresh parsley

Put the bacon into a pan with the water and bay leaf. Blend the carrots, onions, parsnip and cabbage until coarsely chopped. Add to the pan, bring to the boil, cover and simmer gently for 40 minutes. Remove the bacon, cut into small pieces, and blend until finely chopped. Return to the pan with the seasoning and chutney, and bring to the boil.

Meanwhile, mix the flour, suet and sausage-meat. Chop the parsley finely and add to the mixture. Form into 10 balls and add to the soup. Cover and simmer for 15 minutes.

Ham and Green Pea Soup

1 ham hock bone
1 medium onion
1 small carrot
1.8 litres/3 pints water
350g/12 oz dried peas
salt and pepper
a pinch of dried sage

Put the hock bone into a large pan. Blend the onion and carrot until coarsely chopped, then add to the pan with the water, bring to the boil, cover and simmer for 1½ hours. Take out the hock bone and remove the meat. Return to the pan. Blend the dried peas until finely chopped and add to the pan. Bring to the boil, cover and simmer for 1 hour. Blend the soup until smooth. Season to taste with salt, pepper and sage, and re-heat before serving.

Pork and Cabbage Soup

225g/8 oz salt pork
100g/4 oz onions
25g/1 oz dripping
1.5 litres/2½ pints beef stock
1 small cabbage
1 medium carrot
1 stick of celery
pepper

Soak the pork in salted water for 30 minutes. Drain, then cut into small pieces. Blend the onions finely until chopped. Heat the dripping, and fry the onions until soft and golden. Add the pork and stock, and simmer for 30 minutes. Cut the cabbage in pieces and blend until coarsely chopped. Add to the soup. Blend the carrot and celery until finely chopped, and add to the soup. Season well with pepper. Simmer for 30 minutes and adjust the seasoning before serving.

Scotch Broth

450g/1 lb lean neck of mutton **or** lamb
25g/1 oz pearl barley
1.8 litres/3 pints water
1 leek
2 celery sticks
1 medium onion
1 medium carrot
1 medium turnip
salt and pepper

GARNISH
1 × 15ml spoon/1 tablespoon chopped parsley

Cut the meat into small pieces and put into a large pan with the barley and water. Bring slowly to the boil, cover and simmer for 1 hour. Blend the vegetables until coarsely chopped, and add to the stock. Simmer for 1½ hours, then skim. Lift out the pieces of meat, and blend until finely chopped. Return to the pan and re-heat. Season to taste and sprinkle with chopped parsley.

Creamed Fish Soup

1 small onion
300ml/½ pint water
350g/12 oz white fish (see **Note**)
25g/1 oz butter
1 × 15ml spoon/1 tablespoon fresh parsley
25g/1 oz plain flour
300ml/½ pint milk
salt and pepper

GARNISH
peeled shrimps

Blend the onions until chopped, and put into the water with the fish. Cover and simmer until just soft. Blend until smooth with the cooking liquid, butter, parsley, flour and milk. Heat gently, stirring until smooth and hot. Season to taste and garnish with shrimps.

Note The fish can be a mixture of white fish; a little smoked haddock may be included.

Crab Chowder

4 lean bacon rashers, without rinds
25g/1 oz plain flour
600ml/1 pint milk
300ml/½ pint tomato juice
a pinch of basil
a pinch of marjoram
a pinch of pepper
a pinch of garlic powder
175g/6 oz cooked potatoes
450g/1 lb crabmeat
150ml/¼ pint single cream

Fry the bacon without added fat until crisp. Drain, then break into small pieces. Blend until coarsely chopped and put to one side. Blend the bacon fat with the flour, milk, tomato juice, herbs and seasonings until smooth. Put into a large pan and simmer for 5 minutes, stirring well. Chop the potatoes coarsely in the blender and add to the soup with the crabmeat. Simmer for 10 minutes. Adjust the seasoning if necessary. Stir in the cream and re-heat gently without boiling. Serve sprinkled with the reserved bacon pieces.

Main Courses and Salads

Chicken in Curry Sauce

4 chicken pieces
600ml/1 pint water
2 medium onions
25g/1 oz butter
25g/1 oz curry powder
15g/½ oz cornflour
1 × 15ml spoon/1 tablespoon vinegar
15g/½ oz soft brown sugar
1 × 15ml spoon/1 tablespoon sweet chutney
25g/1 oz sultanas

Simmer the chicken pieces in the water until tender. Drain off the stock, reserving it in a bowl, and keep the chicken warm. Blend the onions until coarsely chopped. Melt the butter in a pan and cook the onions until soft but not brown. Add the curry powder and cook for 1 minute. Blend the reserved chicken stock and the cornflour with the vinegar, sugar and chutney until smooth, then add to the onions, and simmer for 5 minutes. Add the chicken pieces and the sultanas, and simmer for 15 minutes. Serve on a bed of rice.

Chicken and Ham Loaf

175g/6 oz cooked chicken
175g/6 oz cooked ham
1 small onion
300ml/½ pint milk
a pinch of nutmeg
salt and pepper
25g/1 oz plain flour
25g/1 oz softened butter
2 × 5ml spoons/2 teaspoons parsley
1 × 2.5ml spoon/½ teaspoon made mustard
1 × 2.5ml spoon/½ teaspoon Worcestershire sauce

Cut the chicken and ham into pieces, blend until finely chopped, and put into a bowl. Blend the onion until smooth with the milk, nutmeg, salt and pepper, flour and butter, then cook gently until thick. Blend with the chicken and ham, the parsley, mustard and Worcestershire sauce until well mixed but not smooth. Put into a 675g/1½ lb loaf tin and chill for 1 hour. Turn out and serve with salad.

Chicken Mousse

350ml/12fl oz chicken stock
25g/1 oz gelatine
salt and pepper
1 thin slice of onion
2 eggs
50g/2 oz almonds
225g/8 oz cooked chicken
250ml/8fl oz double cream

Bring the stock to the boil, and blend half with the gelatine, salt, pepper and onion until smooth. Blend on high speed with the eggs, almonds and coarsely chopped chicken, gradually adding the cream until the mixture is smooth. Pour into a 900ml/1½ pint mould and chill until set.

Honeyed Almond Roast Chicken

1.4–1.8kg/3–4 lb chicken
1 × 15ml spoon/1 tablespoon oil
a pinch of salt
a sprig of rosemary

STUFFING
25g/1 oz dried apricots
25g/1 oz blanched almonds
1 small onion
25g/1 oz butter
50g/2 oz white bread
1 × 2.5ml spoon/½ teaspoon thyme
1 × 15ml spoon/1 tablespoon clear honey
1 egg

To make the stuffing, soak the apricots in water for 3 hours, then drain. Blend with the almonds on low speed until the almonds are finely chopped. Put into a bowl. Blend the onion until chopped, then cook in the butter until soft and golden. Add to the bowl. Break the bread into pieces and make into breadcrumbs in the blender, mixing the bread with the thyme. Add to the bowl with the honey. Mix together and add about half the egg to make a light crumbly stuffing.

Put the stuffing in the neck of the bird under the skin flap. Brush the chicken with the oil, sprinkle with salt and put the sprig of rosemary on top. Cover with foil and bake at 200°C/400°F/Gas 6, allowing 20 minutes per 0.5kg/1 lb + 20 minutes extra. Remove the foil 15 minutes before the end of the cooking time to allow the bird to brown.

Chicken Vol-au-vents

25g/1 oz butter
25g/1 oz plain flour
150ml/¼ pint chicken stock
150ml/¼ pint milk
225g/8 oz cooked chicken
1 small green pepper
2 × 15ml spoons/2 tablespoons single cream
1 × 2.5ml spoon/½ teaspoon Tabasco sauce
salt and pepper
12 × 7.5cm/3 inch baked vol-au-vent cases

Melt the butter. Blend the flour, chicken stock and milk until smooth, then pour on to the butter and stir over gentle heat until the mixture boils. Simmer for 2 minutes, stirring well. Blend with the chicken cut in pieces, the green pepper, cream, Tabasco sauce, salt and pepper until the chicken is finely chopped. Return to the saucepan and simmer for 8 minutes.

Fill the vol-au-vent cases with the mixture, and serve hot.

Variation

Add a few mushrooms to the mixture, or substitute ham or seafood for the chicken.

Beef Fritters

450g/1 lb raw minced beef
1 medium onion
1 × 2.5ml spoon/½ teaspoon mixed herbs
1 × 15ml spoon/1 tablespoon concentrated tomato purée
1 × 15ml spoon/1 tablespoon French mustard
salt and pepper

BATTER
100g/4 oz plain flour
½ × 2.5ml spoon/¼ teaspoon salt
1 egg
6 × 15ml spoons/6 tablespoons beer

Make the batter first. Blend the flour, salt, egg and beer until thick and creamy (it is best to put the flour into the blender last).

Mix together very thoroughly the beef, grated onion, herbs, tomato purée, mustard, salt and pepper and divide into eight pieces. Shape into balls and press out into thin rounds on a floured surface. Dip into the batter and fry in hot fat or oil for 15 minutes, turning once. Drain well on absorbent paper and serve with tomato sauce.

Note The batter can be made with milk, but beer gives a light crisp fritter.

Beef Olives

450g/1 lb braising steak
1 large onion
25g/1 oz dripping
75g/3 oz fresh white bread
grated rind and juice of ½ lemon
1 egg
salt and pepper
1 × 2.5ml spoon/½ teaspoon sage
300ml/½ pint stock
15g/½ oz cornflour

Cut the steak into four slices and flatten them with a rolling-pin. Blend the onion until finely chopped, then cook lightly in the dripping. Break the bread into pieces and make into breadcrumbs in the blender. Add the grated lemon rind and juice, the egg, salt, pepper and sage, and blend until well mixed. Divide the mixture between the pieces of steak and roll up each steak around the stuffing, tying with cotton. Remove the onion from the fat and brown the meat rolls in the remaining fat. Return the onion to the pan, add the stock, cover and simmer for 1½ hours. Put the meat rolls on a serving dish. Mix the cornflour with a little water, stir into the stock, and cook for 3 minutes, stirring well. Pour over the beef olives.

Sweet and Sour Pork

675g/$1\frac{1}{2}$lb lean pork
juice of $\frac{1}{2}$ lemon
fat for deep frying

BATTER
1 egg
100g/4oz plain flour
150ml/$\frac{1}{4}$ pint milk
salt and pepper

Cut the pork into 2.5cm/1 inch cubes and leave in a bowl with the lemon juice for 30 minutes.

To make the batter, blend the egg, flour, milk and seasoning until creamy and smooth.

Drain the pork pieces, dip in the batter and deep fry until golden-brown and crisp. Drain on kitchen paper and serve with Sweet and Sour Sauce (page 39).

Stuffed Liver

350g/12oz lamb's **or** pig's liver
50g/2oz fresh white bread
1 small onion
a sprig of parsley
1 size 7 egg
1 × 2.5ml spoon/$\frac{1}{2}$ teaspoon Worcestershire sauce
6 rashers streaky bacon, without rinds
300ml/$\frac{1}{2}$ pint stock

Cut the liver into thin slices and put into a greased ovenproof dish. Break the bread into small pieces and make into breadcrumbs in the blender. Slice the onion and blend with the parsley, egg and Worcestershire sauce until the parsley is chopped finely. Add this mixture to the breadcrumbs in a bowl, and mix well. Put this stuffing on top of the liver slices, and cover with bacon rashers. Pour on the stock. Bake at 180°C/350°F/Gas 4 for 40 minutes until tender.

Apricot Pork with Apple Sauce

1.8kg/4lb boned pork joint
350g/12oz cooking apples
25g/1oz Demerara sugar

STUFFING
100g/4oz white bread
a sprig of parsley
425g/15oz canned apricot halves
1 × 2.5ml spoon/$\frac{1}{2}$ teaspoon fresh mixed herbs
1 egg
salt and pepper

Make the stuffing first. Break the bread into pieces and make into breadcrumbs in the blender, adding the parsley with the last batch of bread. Put into a mixing bowl. Drain the apricots, reserving the syrup, and blend half the fruit until roughly chopped. Mix with the bread, herbs, egg and seasoning, and stir well.

Stuff the meat and put it into a roasting tin. Pour over the reserved syrup and cook at 190°C/375°F/Gas 5 for $2\frac{1}{2}$ hours, basting with syrup once or twice.

Peel and core the apples and blend until roughly chopped. Put into a saucepan with 6 × 15ml spoons/6 tablespoons water and the Demerara sugar, and cook until soft. Blend with the remaining apricots until smooth, and re-heat just before serving with the pork.

Apricot Pork with Apple Sauce

Bakehouse Lamb

675g/1½lb potatoes
225g/8oz onions
salt and pepper
1.8kg/4lb leg of lamb
4 × 15ml spoons/4 tablespoons mint jelly
100g/4oz day-old white bread
2 large sprigs parsley

Slice the potatoes. Blend the onions until coarsely chopped. Arrange half the potatoes in a layer on the base of a greased ovenproof dish. Season with salt and pepper. Sprinkle with the onions and then put in the remaining potatoes. Place the leg of lamb on top of this bed of vegetables. Do not add any fat as there will be enough in the lamb for roasting the meat and vegetables. Sprinkle the skin of the lamb with salt and pepper. Roast at 190°C/375°F/Gas 5 for 1 hour. Baste the vegetables with the fat from the lamb. Spread the mint jelly on the lamb skin.

Discard the crusts, break the bread into pieces and make into crumbs in the blender, mixing with the parsley. Season with salt and pepper and press all over the skin of the lamb. Sprinkle a little fat on the crumbs. Continue roasting for 45 minutes. Remove the lamb to a carving dish and serve the vegetables from the ovenproof dish.

Pennywise Lamb Roast

1 breast of lamb
2 × 5ml spoons/2 teaspoons made mustard

STUFFING
100g/4oz soft white bread
1 × 15ml spoon/1 tablespoon fresh mint **or** parsley
1 × 2.5ml spoon/½ teaspoon mixed herbs
1 small onion
salt and pepper
1 egg

Remove the bones from the lamb, or get the butcher to do this. Score any skin with a sharp knife, cutting just through the skin and no deeper. Spread the mustard over the meat.

To make the stuffing, break the bread in small pieces and make into crumbs in the blender. Put into a bowl. Blend the mint or parsley, herbs and roughly chopped onion with the seasoning and egg until the onion is finely chopped. Pour on to the breadcrumbs and mix well.

Spread the stuffing over the meat and roll it up, tying securely. Brown on all sides in a little hot fat. Bake at 200°C/400°F/Gas 6 for 15 minutes, then at 180°C/350°F/Gas 4 for 1¼ hours.

Serve with a rich brown gravy and oven-baked jacket potatoes.

Note Boiled butter beans or haricot beans dressed with butter and chopped parsley are also good with lamb.

Fish Cakes

450g/1 lb cooked fish
2 size 1–2 eggs
25g/1 oz plain flour
2 × 15ml spoons/2 tablespoons lemon juice
2 × 15ml spoons/2 tablespoons parsley
1 × 5ml spoon/1 teaspoon Worcestershire sauce
40g/1½ oz melted butter
salt and pepper
450g/1 lb mashed potatoes
beaten egg
breadcrumbs

Break the fish into small pieces and blend with the eggs, flour, lemon juice, parsley, Worcestershire sauce, butter and seasoning. Blend until the fish is well broken up. Work the mixture into the mashed potatoes. Divide into 16 pieces and make into round flat cakes. Coat with beaten eggs and breadcrumbs, and fry until golden-brown.

Fish Puffs

150ml/¼ pint lukewarm water
1 × 15ml spoon/1 tablespoon oil
100g/4 oz plain flour
a pinch of salt
225g/8 oz flaked cooked fish (see **Note**)
1 × 15ml spoon/1 tablespoon lemon juice
25g/1 oz capers
2 egg whites
fat for deep frying

Blend the water, oil, flour and salt until thick and creamy. Add the fish, lemon juice and capers, and blend until well mixed. Whisk the egg whites until stiff, and fold into the fish mixture. Put spoonfuls into hot fat and deep fry until the puffs are golden-brown and crisp.

Note Fish puffs can be made with cod, haddock or salmon.

Stuffed Whole Plaice

2 small whole plaice

STUFFING
1 small onion
50g/2 oz mushrooms
25g/1 oz butter
50g/2 oz fresh white bread
salt and pepper

GARNISH
lemon slices
parsley

To make the stuffing, blend the onion and mushrooms until finely chopped. Melt the butter in a pan and cook the onion and mushrooms until the onion is soft but not coloured. Break the bread into pieces and make into breadcrumbs in the blender. Mix with the onion, mushrooms, salt and pepper.

Skin the fish and make a cut down the centre of one side of each. Fill with the stuffing, and put in a greased ovenproof dish. Bake at 200°C/400°F/Gas 6 for 30 minutes. Garnish with lemon slices and parsley.

Baked Stuffed Mackerel

4 mackerel

STUFFING
1 onion
25g/1 oz butter
1 apple
75g/3 oz fresh white bread
1 × 2.5ml spoon/½ teaspoon mixed herbs
grated rind and juice of ½ lemon
salt and pepper

GARNISH
lemon slices
sprigs parsley

Make the stuffing first. Blend the onion until finely chopped. Melt the butter in a pan and cook the vegetables until soft but not coloured. Peel the apple and blend until chopped. Break the bread into pieces and make into breadcrumbs in the blender. Mix together with the onion, apple, herbs, lemon rind and juice, salt and pepper.

Open each fish and press out the backbone. Divide the stuffing between the fish, and roll up from the wide end, securing with a cocktail stick. Put in an ovenproof dish and brush each fish with a little oil. Cover with a piece of foil or a lid and bake at 180°C/350°F/Gas 4 for 30 minutes. Remove the foil or lid and continue cooking for 5 minutes. Garnish with lemon slices and sprigs of parsley.

Serve with thin brown bread and butter.

Salmon Mousse

450g/1 lb canned pink salmon
25g/1 oz butter
25g/1 oz plain flour
300ml/½ pint milk
salt and pepper
3 × 15ml spoons/3 tablespoons tomato ketchup
1 × 5ml spoon/1 teaspoon anchovy essence
1 × 2.5ml spoon/½ teaspoon lemon juice
15g/½ oz gelatine
2 × 15ml spoons/2 tablespoons water
150ml/¼ pint double cream
2 egg whites

GARNISH
cucumber slices
stuffed olives

Prepare a 15cm/6 inch soufflé dish by tying a band of paper or foil round the outside so that it comes about 5cm/2 inches above the top of the dish.

Drain the salmon and remove skin and bones. Mash the salmon lightly with a fork. Melt the butter in a pan, stir in the flour and cook gently for 1 minute. Add the milk and bring to the boil, stirring all the time. Simmer for 3 minutes and season with salt and pepper. Cool slightly and blend with the salmon, tomato ketchup, anchovy essence and lemon juice. Stir the gelatine into the water and heat in a bowl over hot water until the gelatine is syrupy. Blend with the fish until smooth and creamy. Whip the cream to soft peaks and fold into the salmon mixture. Whisk the egg whites to stiff peaks, fold in the salmon mixture and pour into the soufflé dish. Leave in a cold place until set, and remove the paper collar carefully. Garnish with thin slices of cucumber and stuffed olives.

Salmon Mousse

BRAUN

QUICHE LORRAINE

225g/8 oz prepared shortcrust pastry
1 medium onion
50g/2 oz streaky bacon, without rinds
25g/1 oz butter
2 eggs and 2 egg yolks
225ml/7fl oz creamy milk
pepper
100g/4 oz cheese

Roll out the pastry and use to line a 20cm/8 inch flan ring or dish. Cut the onion and bacon in pieces. Blend until finely chopped, then cook until soft in the butter. Put into the pastry case. Blend the eggs, egg yolks, milk and pepper with the cheese cut in small pieces so that the eggs and milk are well mixed together. Pour into the pastry case. Bake at 190°C/375°F/Gas 5 for 35 minutes. Serve hot or cold.

CHEESE CRUMB SOUFFLÉ

3 thick slices white bread
150ml/$\frac{1}{4}$ pint milk
25g/1 oz butter
75g/3 oz Cheddar cheese
2 eggs, separated
salt and pepper

Remove the crusts from the bread, break the bread into pieces, and make into breadcrumbs in the blender. Put into a bowl. Warm the milk and butter until the butter melts. Cut the cheese into small pieces and blend with the warmed milk and egg yolks until smooth. Pour on to the breadcrumbs, and season with salt and pepper. Whisk the egg whites until stiff but not dry. Fold into the cheese mixture, and put into a greased 1.2 litre/2 pint soufflé dish or pie dish. Bake at 200°C/400°F/Gas 6 for 30 minutes. Serve at once.

PLAIN OMELET

2 eggs
2 × 15ml spoons/2 tablespoons water
salt and pepper
butter for frying

FILLINGS
grated cheese **or** cooked vegetables **or** mushrooms **or** ham **or** asparagus **or** creamed poultry **or** kidneys **or** cooked fish

Blend the eggs, water and seasoning until well mixed. Melt a knob of butter in a very hot omelet pan and pour in the mixture. Lower the heat and loosen the bottom of the omelet with a palette knife to allow the uncooked mixture to run underneath. As soon as it is set, put in the filling, fold and serve on a hot plate.

APPLE AND WALNUT SALAD

6 sticks celery
3 eating apples
75g/3 oz walnuts
150ml/$\frac{1}{4}$ pint mayonnaise
5 × 15ml spoons/5 tablespoons double cream
shredded lettuce

Cut the celery into pieces. Without peeling the apples, remove the cores and cut the apples into pieces. Blend with the celery and walnuts until coarsely chopped. Stir together the mayonnaise and double cream, and mix into the apple mixture. Arrange on a bed of shredded lettuce.

Mediterranean Salad

350g/12 oz cooked ham
225g/8 oz cooked rice
1 stick of celery
100g/4 oz button mushrooms
50g/2 oz black olives
100g/4 oz grapes
6 × 15ml spoons/6 tablespoons oil
3 × 15ml spoons/3 tablespoons red wine vinegar
1 clove garlic
1 × 5ml spoon/1 teaspoon salt
1 × 2.5ml spoon/½ teaspoon rosemary
a pinch of pepper
shredded lettuce

Cut the ham into pieces and blend until coarsely chopped. Mix with the rice in a bowl. Cut the celery into pieces and blend until coarsely chopped. Add to the ham and rice. Blend the mushrooms and olives until coarsely chopped and add to the ham and rice. Halve the grapes, remove the seeds, and stir into the mixture. Blend the oil, vinegar, garlic and seasonings until creamy. Pour over the ham and rice mixture, and stir well. Arrange on a bed of shredded lettuce.

Sunshine Salad

4 medium carrots
50g/2 oz salted peanuts
6 × 15ml spoons/6 tablespoons mayonnaise
lettuce leaves
4 pineapple rings

Cut the carrots into small pieces. Blend with the peanuts until finely chopped, and mix with the mayonnaise. Arrange a bed of lettuce leaves on a serving plate and spoon on the carrot mixture. Chop the pineapple rings coarsely and blend until finely chopped. Spoon over the salad mixture, and serve at once.

Winter Chicken Salad

350g/12 oz cooked chicken
3 sticks celery
4 eating apples
2 × 15ml spoons/2 tablespoons lemon juice
75g/3 oz walnut kernels
150ml/¼ pint mayonnaise
4 × 15ml spoons/4 tablespoons double cream
chicory **or** lettuce leaves

Cut the chicken into pieces and blend until coarsely chopped. Put into a bowl. Cut the celery into pieces and blend until coarsely chopped. Add to the chicken. Do not peel the apples, but cut them into quarters and remove the cores. Blend until coarsely chopped and toss in the lemon juice. Blend the walnuts until coarsely chopped. Mix together the chicken, celery, apples and walnuts in the bowl. Stir together the mayonnaise and cream and mix into the chicken. Serve on a bed of chicory or lettuce.

Sauces, Dressings and Stuffings

Apple Sauce

450g/1 lb cooking apples
4 × 15ml spoons/4 tablespoons water
sugar
25g/1 oz butter

Core the apples but do not peel them. Cut in pieces and put into a pan with the water. Simmer until soft, and add sugar to taste. Blend with the butter on medium speed until smooth.

Note The sauce should not be too sweet if served with meat or poultry.

Brown Sauce

1 onion
1 carrot
15g/½ oz butter
300ml/½ pint brown stock
salt and pepper
15g/½ oz plain flour

Cut the onion into pieces with the carrot, then blend until finely chopped. Melt the butter in a pan and cook the vegetables until soft but not coloured. Add the stock, salt and pepper, and simmer for 30 minutes. Blend with the flour until smooth. Bring to the boil, stirring well, and cook for 3 minutes.

Barbecue Sauce

1 medium onion
25g/1 oz butter
15g/½ oz plain flour
2 × 5ml spoons/2 teaspoons French mustard
1 × 2.5ml spoon/½ teaspoon mustard powder
1 × 15ml spoon/1 tablespoon Worcestershire sauce
1 × 5ml spoon/1 teaspoon Tabasco sauce
15g/½ oz brown sugar
1 × 5ml spoon/1 teaspoon salt
1 × 15ml spoon/1 tablespoon vinegar
250ml/8fl oz tomato juice

Cut the onion into pieces, and blend until finely chopped. Melt the butter in a pan and cook until golden. Stir in the flour and cook for 2 minutes. Blend with the remaining ingredients until smooth. Bring to boiling point, then simmer for 5 minutes, stirring well.

Bread Sauce with Onion

1 small onion
300ml/½ pint milk
a pinch of ground cloves
100g/4 oz day-old white bread
25g/1 oz butter
salt and pepper
2 × 15ml spoons/2 tablespoons single cream

Blend the onion until finely chopped. Put into a pan with the milk and cloves and bring slowly to boiling point. Leave to stand in a warm place for 30 minutes. Break the bread into pieces and make into breadcrumbs in the blender. Stir the crumbs into the milk, and simmer for 5 minutes. Stir in the butter, salt, pepper and cream, and serve at once.

Note This is more strongly flavoured than the usual bread sauce and is very good with chicken, game or sausages.

Cranberry Apple Sauce

450g/1 lb cooking apples
450g/1 lb cranberries
600ml/1 pint water
175g/6 oz sugar

Peel and core the apples, and blend with the cranberries in small quantities with the water, until finely chopped. Add the sugar, and simmer over low heat until the fruit is soft. Blend until smooth.

Serve with pork or turkey.

Curry Sauce

1 onion
1 × 15ml spoon/1 tablespoon oil
25g/1 oz plain flour
15g/½ oz curry powder
1 × 5ml spoon/1 teaspoon curry paste
450ml/¾ pint beef **or** chicken stock
1 eating apple
50g/2 oz sultanas
2 × 5ml spoons/2 teaspoons lemon juice
salt and pepper

Blend the onion until finely chopped. Cook over low heat in the oil until soft and golden. Stir in the flour, curry powder and paste, and continue cooking for 3 minutes. Add the stock and simmer over low heat for 10 minutes. Peel and core the apple and blend until finely chopped. Add to the sauce with the sultanas, lemon juice and seasoning. Simmer for 10 minutes. If a smooth sauce is preferred, blend before adding the sultanas and seasonings.

Serve with cooked meat, poultry, fish, seafood or eggs.

Flavoured Butters

Flavoured butters are useful as spreads for bread or pancakes, as a base for sandwiches, and as dressings for meat and fish. The butter should be at room temperature, and blended at low speed until smooth, stopping the machine to scrape down if necessary. Additions such as nuts or herbs should be made only when the butter is well creamed, and the blender should then be run on high speed just until the additions are coarsely chopped.

Garlic Butter
Add 1 garlic clove and a pinch of salt to 100g/4 oz butter. Use for rolls, French bread or grilled meat.
Honey Butter
Add 4 × 15ml spoons/4 tablespoons liquid honey and a pinch of salt to 100g/4 oz butter. Use for toast or biscuits.
Maple Butter
Add 4 × 15ml spoons/4 tablespoons maple syrup, 2 × 15ml spoons/2 tablespoons liquid honey and 50g/2 oz walnuts to 100g/4 oz butter. Use for pancakes or waffles.
Parsley Butter
Add 6 sprigs parsley and a squeeze of lemon juice to 100g/4 oz butter. Use for grilled meat or fish.
Watercress Butter
And ½ bunch washed and dried watercress, a pinch of salt, 1 × 15ml spoon/1 tablespoon lemon juice and a pinch of celery seed to 100g/4 oz butter. Use for grilled meat or fish.

Hollandaise Sauce

3 egg yolks
1 × 15ml spoon/1 tablespoon lemon juice
1 × 15ml spoon/1 tablespoon warm water
salt and white pepper
100g/4 oz unsalted butter

Blend the egg yolks, lemon juice, water, salt and pepper. Melt the butter without browning. With the machine running, pour the butter slowly through the lid until completely mixed in and the sauce is thick.

Serve immediately with fish, asparagus, artichokes or other vegetables.

Variations

Aurora Sauce
Fold 3 × 15ml spoons/3 tablespoons mayonnaise and 150ml/¼ pint whipped cream into the Hollandaise sauce, and serve with cold chicken or fish.

Maltaise Sauce
Stir in 1 × 5ml spoon/1 teaspoon grated orange rind and 1 × 15ml spoon/1 tablespoon orange juice and serve with vegetables.

Mousseline Sauce
Before preparing the Hollandaise Sauce, whip 150ml/¼ pint double cream to soft peaks and keep on one side. Prepare the sauce and fold in the cream. Serve with fish, vegetables or eggs.

Horseradish Cream Sauce

2 spring onions
150ml/¼ pint double cream
1 × 15ml spoon/1 tablespoon lemon juice
1 × 5ml spoon/1 teaspoon horseradish sauce
2 × 5ml spoon/2 teaspoons Worcestershire sauce

Cut the white part and a little of the green of the onions into pieces. Blend with the cream, lemon juice, horseradish sauce and Worcestershire sauce until the onions are very finely chopped. Chill and serve with steak, roast beef, hamburgers or jacket potatoes.

Indonesian Sauce

1 × 15ml spoon/1 tablespoon salad oil
4 × 15ml spoons/4 tablespoons peanut butter
150ml/¼ pint tomato sauce
3 × 15ml spoons/3 tablespoons Worcestershire sauce
1 clove garlic
a large pinch of salt

Heat the oil gently in a pan and stir in the peanut butter. Continue heating gently, stirring occasionally, until the peanut butter begins to thicken and darken slightly. Blend with all the other ingredients until smooth and leave to stand for 2 hours before using. Re-heat gently and serve with chicken, steak or kebabs.

Note If the sauce is rather thick, blend in a little water before re-heating.

Rich Mushroom Sauce

1 medium onion
15g/½oz butter
175g/6oz mushrooms
150ml/¼ pint red wine
150ml/¼ pint beef stock
15g/½oz cornflour
1 × 15ml spoon/1 tablespoon Worcestershire sauce
salt and pepper

Cut the onion in pieces and blend until finely chopped. Melt the butter in a pan and fry the onion until soft. Cut the mushrooms in pieces and blend with the wine and stock until the mushrooms are finely chopped. Return to the pan and simmer for 10 minutes. Blend some of the sauce with the cornflour, Worcestershire sauce, salt and pepper until smooth. Return to the pan with the remaining sauce, and simmer for 5 minutes.

Note This sauce is very good with roast beef or steak, and with poultry.

Sweet Devil Sauce

3 × 15ml spoons/3 tablespoons vinegar
75g/3oz soft brown sugar
1 × 15ml spoon/1 tablespoon olive oil
1 clove garlic
40g/1½oz mustard powder
a pinch of salt

Heat the vinegar and blend with the sugar, oil, chopped garlic, mustard powder and salt until smooth and creamy. Put into a bowl, cover and leave to stand for 24 hours before using with boiled beef, tongue or ham.

Sweet and Sour Sauce

3 canned pineapple rings
1 small onion
40g/1½oz sugar
15g/½oz cornflour
2 × 15ml spoons/2 tablespoons vinegar
2 × 5ml spoons/2 teaspoons soy sauce
2 × 5ml spoons/2 teaspoons concentrated tomato purée
a pinch of salt
300ml/½ pint water

Cut the pineapple into pieces and blend with the onion until finely chopped. Put to one side. Blend the sugar, cornflour, vinegar, soy sauce, tomato purée, salt and water until smooth, then simmer gently over low heat, stirring until the sauce thickens. Add the onion and pineapple, and continue simmering for 3 minutes.

Serve with pork or chicken.

Tomato Sauce

1 medium onion
1 clove garlic
1 × 15ml spoon/1 tablespoon olive oil
450g/1 lb ripe tomatoes
1 × 5ml spoon/1 teaspoon salt
1 × 5ml spoon/1 teaspoon sugar
1 × 5ml spoon/1 teaspoon paprika
1 × 15ml spoon/1 tablespoon vinegar
1 bay leaf
pepper

Cut the onion into pieces and blend with the garlic until finely chopped. Cook gently in the oil until golden. Skin the tomatoes and blend until coarsely chopped. Add to the onion with the other ingredients and simmer for 15 minutes. Remove the bay leaf and blend the sauce on medium speed until smooth. Put through a sieve, then simmer for 20 minutes.

White Sauce

25g/1 oz melted butter
25g/1 oz plain flour
300ml/$\frac{1}{2}$ pint milk
salt and white pepper

Blend the butter, flour and milk until smooth. Pour into a pan, bring to the boil and simmer for 3 minutes, stirring all the time. Season to taste.

Variations

Blend the additional ingredients until chopped and put into a bowl before making the sauce.

Cheese Sauce
Stir 75g/3 oz grated or chopped cheese into the sauce just before serving.
Egg Sauce
Stir 2 chopped hard-boiled eggs into the cooked sauce.
Onion Sauce
Cook 1 finely chopped medium onion in the sauce. Flavour with a pinch of ground nutmeg.
Parsley Sauce
Stir 2 large chopped sprigs of parsley into the cooked sauce.
Shrimp Sauce
Add 75g/3 oz peeled, finely chopped shrimps to the cooked sauce, and season with a few drops of Tabasco sauce.

Avocado Dressing

1 avocado pear
2 × 15ml spoons/2 tablespoons double cream
2 × 15ml spoons/2 tablespoons lemon juice
1 × 5ml spoon/1 teaspoon made mustard
salt and pepper
a few drops Worcestershire sauce

Peel the avocado and remove the stone. Cut the flesh into small pieces. Blend all the ingredients until smooth and creamy. Serve at once with cold fish or seafood.

Note This dressing should only be made just before serving, or it will discolour.

Mayonnaise

1 size 3–4 egg
1 × 15ml spoon/1 tablespoon vinegar **or** lemon juice
1 × 2.5ml spoon/$\frac{1}{2}$ teaspoon salt
1 × 5ml spoon/1 teaspoon sugar
$\frac{1}{2}$ × 2.5ml spoon/$\frac{1}{4}$ teaspoon mustard powder
$\frac{1}{2}$ × 2.5ml spoon/$\frac{1}{4}$ teaspoon pepper
300ml/$\frac{1}{2}$ pint salad oil

Blend the egg, vinegar or lemon juice, salt, sugar, mustard and pepper on medium speed for 5 seconds. Start to pour the oil gently through the centre section of the cover while the blender is running. Continue blending for about 1 minute until the oil has been incorporated. It may be necessary to stop the blender and scrape down the sides with a spatula. This gives a creamy mixture, but if a thicker mayonnaise is preferred, use 2 egg yolks instead of the whole egg.

Mayonnaise

Devil Dressing

1 orange
1 × 15 ml spoon/1 tablespoon made mustard
2 × 15ml spoons/2 tablespoons redcurrant jelly
1 × 15ml spoon/1 tablespoon grated horseradish

Squeeze the juice from the orange and blend with one thin slice of orange rind and the other ingredients until the rind is very finely chopped. Simmer for 3 minutes and serve hot or cold with ham or pork.

Low-Calorie Dressing

4 × 15ml spoons/4 tablespoons tomato juice
1 thin slice of onion
1 × 5ml spoon/1 teaspoon made mustard
salt and pepper
1 × 15ml spoon/1 tablespoon parsley **or** mint

Blend all the ingredients until the onion and herbs are finely chopped. Use with green salads or vegetable salads.

Variation

Use a mixture of orange and lemon juice, or orange and grapefruit juice instead of tomato juice.

Salad Cream

450ml/¾ pint milk
40g/1½ oz plain flour
40g/1½ oz sugar
2 × 5ml spoons/2 teaspoons mustard powder
50g/2 oz margarine
1 egg
150ml/¼ pint vinegar

Blend the milk with the flour until smooth, then blend in the sugar and mustard powder. Melt the margarine and pour in the liquid. Stir over low heat until thick and creamy. Cool, then blend with the egg until creamy, gradually adding the vinegar through the hole in the lid with the motor running, until it is all absorbed.

Note This will keep for 4 weeks in a cold place.

Soured Cream Dressing

250ml/8fl oz soured cream
2 × 15ml spoons/2 tablespoons vinegar
1 × 15ml spoon/1 tablespoon lemon juice
1 × 2.5ml spoon/½ teaspoon salt
40g/1½ oz sugar
pepper

Blend all the ingredients on minimum speed until creamy and well blended. Serve cold with seafood or salads.

Vinaigrette Sauce

4 × 15ml spoons/4 tablespoons oil
2 × 15ml spoons/2 tablespoons wine vinegar
1 × 2.5ml spoon/½ teaspoon salt
1 × 2.5ml spoon/½ teaspoon caster sugar
1 × 2.5ml spoon/½ teaspoon mustard powder
a pinch of pepper

Blend all the ingredients until smooth. Use for green salads, tomatoes, cold leeks, asparagus, globe artichokes and avocado pears.

Yoghurt Salad Dressing

150ml/¼ pint natural yoghurt
1 × 5ml spoon/1 teaspoon parsley
1 × 5ml spoon/1 teaspoon chives
1 thin slice of onion
1 × 5ml spoon/1 teaspoon made mustard

Blend all the ingredients until the herbs are finely chopped. Serve cold with salads or fish.

Variation

Add a thick slice of cucumber (including the skin).

Apple and Walnut Stuffing

450g/1 lb cooking apples
25g/1 oz walnuts
25g/1 oz sugar
100g/4 oz white bread
1 small onion
1 × 5ml spoon/1 teaspoon salt
pepper
1 egg
50g/2 oz melted butter

Peel and core the apples, cut into pieces and blend with the walnuts until finely chopped. Put into a bowl with the sugar. Break the bread into pieces and make into breadcrumbs in the blender, adding the onion during the final blending until it is finely chopped. Add to the apple and work in the salt and pepper, egg and melted butter.

Use for pork, duck, goose or bacon joints.

Bacon Stuffing

100g/4 oz white bread
100g/4 oz lean bacon, without rinds
1 × 2.5ml spoon/½ teaspoon mustard powder
½ × 2.5ml spoon/¼ teaspoon salt
1 × 2.5ml spoon/½ teaspoon mixed herbs
25g/1 oz butter
4 × 15ml spoons/4 tablespoons milk

Break the bread into pieces and cut the bacon into small pieces. Make breadcrumbs in the blender, adding the bacon gradually until it is chopped finely. Add the mustard, salt and herbs during the final blending. Put into a bowl. Melt together the butter and milk and pour on to the breadcrumbs. Mix well.

Use for stuffing chicken, turkey or veal.

Herb and Lemon Stuffing

100g/4 oz day-old bread
rind of ½ lemon
1 × 15ml spoon/1 tablespoon fresh parsley
1 × 15ml spoon/1 tablespoon fresh thyme
50g/2 oz melted butter
1 egg
salt and pepper

Break the bread into small pieces. Blend a little with pieces of lemon rind and the herbs until the bread forms fine crumbs. Tip the mixture into a bowl and continue blending small quantities of bread to form fine crumbs. Put all the crumbs into the bowl. Blend the butter, egg and seasoning until just mixed. Pour over the crumbs and stir lightly until mixed.

Use for veal or poultry.

Pineapple Stuffing

100g/4 oz white bread
50g/2 oz cooked lean ham
4 pineapple chunks
1 small onion
salt and pepper
25g/1 oz butter
4 × 15ml spoons/4 tablespoons milk

Break the bread into small pieces and make into breadcrumbs in the blender. During the final blending, add the ham, pineapple and onion cut in pieces, and blend until finely chopped. Put into a bowl, and season with salt and pepper. Heat together the butter and milk and stir into the stuffing.

Use for pork or poultry.

Sage and Onion Stuffing

2 large onions
300ml/½ pint water
50g/2 oz day-old bread
2 × 5ml spoons/2 teaspoons fresh sage leaves
25g/1 oz melted butter
salt and pepper

Cut the onions in pieces and blend with the water until the onions are coarsely chopped. Simmer for 20 minutes, and drain off the cooking liquid, but keep it in reserve. Break the bread into small pieces and blend in small quantities with the sage until the bread forms fine breadcrumbs. Mix the crumbs, sage, melted butter, seasoning, onions and enough cooking liquid to give a moist texture.

Use for duck, goose or pork, or for hearts.

Celery and Apricot Stuffing

175g/6 oz day-old white bread
100g/4 oz apricots
2 sticks celery
50g/2 oz melted butter
salt and pepper

Break the bread into small pieces and make into coarse breadcrumbs in the blender. Put into a bowl. Cover the apricots with cold water, bring to the boil and simmer for 5 minutes. Blend both the apricots and their cooking liquid with the celery cut into pieces until the apricots and celery are coarsely chopped. Pour over the breadcrumbs and stir in the butter, salt and pepper. Mix well and use for poultry or pork.

Basic Poultry Stuffing

1 small loaf day-old bread
1 medium onion
3 × 15ml spoons/3 tablespoons parsley
1 × 15ml spoon/1 tablespoon thyme
50g/2 oz melted butter
salt and pepper
1 × 5ml spoon/1 teaspoon lemon juice

Break the bread into pieces and make into breadcrumbs in the blender. Put the crumbs into a bowl. Cut the onion in pieces. Blend with the remaining ingredients, until the herbs are finely chopped. Pour on to the breadcrumbs and stir until well mixed.

Note An egg may be added for a more solid stuffing. This is enough for a bird weighing 1.8kg/4 lb

Variations

Giblet Stuffing
The giblets of the bird can be cooked, and the liver, heart and meat from the neck added to the herbs and butter to be finely chopped before adding to the breadcrumbs.
Raisin and Nut Stuffing
Chop 100g/4 oz walnut halves and 175g/6 oz seedless raisins in the blender and add to the other ingredients. Use for poultry or pork.

Prune Stuffing

450g/1 lb prunes
red wine
1 lemon
225g/8 oz fresh pork
1 small onion
12 green olives, stoned
50g/2 oz butter
salt and pepper
a pinch of nutmeg
a pinch of thyme
2 eggs

Soak the prunes in cold water for 4 hours. Drain and put into a pan with red wine to cover and the lemon cut in thin slices. Simmer until the prunes are tender. Drain and stone the fruit and blend until coarsely chopped. Mince the pork. Cut the onion in pieces and blend with the olives until finely chopped. Add to the minced pork, and cook in the butter over gentle heat until the pork is cooked but not brown. Season to taste with salt, pepper, nutmeg and thyme, cool slightly and mix with the eggs and the chopped prunes. Chill completely and use to stuff goose or duck.

Pâtés, Spreads and Dips

Seafood Pâté

450g/1 lb fresh prawns **or** shrimps
450g/1 lb haddock
50g/2 oz softened butter
1 × 5ml spoon/1 teaspoon anchovy essence
a pinch of ground mace
a pinch of Cayenne pepper
100g/4 oz clarified butter

Shell the prawns or shrimps and put the shells into a saucepan. Add just enough liquid to cover, and bring to the boil. Strain the liquid and put into a saucepan. Discard the shells. Cut the haddock in pieces and add to the liquid. Simmer for 10 minutes until tender. Blend the prawns or shrimps until coarsely chopped and put into a bowl. Drain the haddock and break into large flakes. Blend with the butter, anchovy essence, mace and Cayenne pepper until smooth. Add to the prawns or shrimps and stir in until well mixed (the creamy fish mixture should be stuffed with large pieces of pink shellfish). Put into a serving dish. Chill for 1 hour. Melt the clarified butter and pour it over the chilled mixture. Chill for 1 hour before serving with toast.

Kipper Pâté

225g/8 oz kipper fillets
25g/1 oz melted butter
juice of ½ lemon
1 clove garlic
1 × 15ml spoon/1 tablespoon brandy
4 drops Tabasco sauce
2 × 15ml spoons/2 tablespoons single cream

Cook the kippers by grilling or poaching them. Remove the skin and larger bones. Break the flesh and blend with the melted butter, lemon juice, garlic clove, brandy and Tabasco sauce until smooth. Add the cream, and blend for 2 seconds. Put into a serving dish and chill before serving.

Sardine Pâté

100g/4 oz canned sardines
125g/5 oz full-fat soft cheese
salt and pepper
1 × 15ml spoon/1 tablespoon lemon juice
2 hard-boiled eggs

Blend the sardines and their oil with the cream cheese cut in pieces, the salt, pepper and lemon juice until just mixed. Cut the eggs in pieces and blend with the other ingredients until the eggs are finely chopped. Put into a serving dish and chill before serving.

SMOKED FISH PÂTÉ

2 smoked trout **or** mackerel
150ml/¼ pint soured cream
100g/4 oz cottage cheese
juice of ½ lemon
salt and pepper

Skin the fish and remove the flesh. Blend with the other ingredients until smooth. Put into small individual dishes, and chill.

Serve with thin slices of toast made from brown bread, and with slices of lemon.

SMOKED SALMON PÂTÉ

450g/1 lb smoked salmon trimmings
50g/2 oz unsalted butter
1 × 15ml spoon/1 tablespoon dry sherry
1 × 15ml spoon/1 tablespoon lemon juice
a pinch of pepper
150ml/¼ pint double cream

Cut the salmon in small pieces. Blend with the butter, sherry, lemon juice and pepper for 10 seconds. Scrape down the mixture and pour in the cream. Blend for 5 seconds. Put into an oiled dish, and chill before serving.

CHICKEN LIVER AND CIDER PÂTÉ

300ml/½ pint dry cider
1 small onion
225g/8 oz chicken liver
25g/1 oz day-old white bread
salt and pepper
a pinch of thyme

GARNISH
chopped parsley

Put the cider into a pan. Cut the onion and liver into small pieces. Put the onion into the cider and simmer until soft. Add the liver and cook gently for 10 minutes. Strain and reserve the liquid. Break the bread into small pieces and make into breadcrumbs in the blender. Put to one side. Blend the onion and liver with 3 × 15ml spoons/3 tablespoons cooking liquid until finely chopped. Add salt, pepper and thyme. Boil the remaining liquid until 2 × 15ml spoons/2 tablespoons remain. Add to the goblet with the crumbs, and blend until creamy. Press the mixture into a serving dish. Sprinkle with chopped parsley. Chill before serving with toast.

Chicken Liver Pâté

225g/8 oz chicken liver
75g/3 oz fat bacon, without rinds
1 small onion
butter
2 cloves garlic
1 egg
salt and pepper

Cut the chicken liver, bacon and onion into pieces. Blend the liver until finely chopped. Put to one side. Blend the bacon and onion until finely chopped. Melt the butter in a pan and cook the bacon and onion until just soft. Add the liver, and cook gently for 10 minutes. Blend with the garlic, egg and seasoning until smooth. Put in a 675g/1½ lb greased ovenproof container and cover with a lid or piece of foil. Stand the container in a roasting tin of water. Cook at 180°C/350°F/Gas 4 for 1 hour. Remove the lid, cover and weight the pâté. Cover the surface with a little melted butter.

Serve with crisp toast.

Chicken and Bacon Pâté

175g/6 oz cooked chicken
4 bacon rashers, without rinds
1 small onion
75g/3 oz full fat soft cheese
1 × 2.5ml spoon/½ teaspoon mixed herbs
salt and pepper
sherry **or** milk

Cut the chicken into pieces. Grill the bacon and cut into pieces. Cut the onion into pieces. Blend all the ingredients until smooth. If the mixture is a little stiff to blend, add a little sherry or milk. Put into a serving dish and chill before serving.

Turkey Terrine

350g/12 oz cooked turkey
2 × 15ml spoons/2 tablespoons brandy
225g/8 oz fat pork
4 × 15ml spoons/4 tablespoons milk
100g/4 oz white bread
1 onion
25g/1 oz butter
1 egg
salt and pepper
a pinch of ground nutmeg
a pinch of dried mixed herbs

Cut the turkey into small pieces and blend until coarsely chopped. Put into a bowl with the brandy and leave to stand while processing the other ingredients. Cut the pork into small pieces and blend with the milk. Put to one side. Cut the bread into pieces and make into breadcrumbs in the blender. Cut the onion into quarters and blend until finely chopped. Melt the butter in a pan and cook the onion until soft and golden. Mix the onion and butter with the pork. Blend the crumbs with the pork, onion, butter, egg, salt, pepper, nutmeg and herbs. Put half the mixture in a 900g/2 lb greased ovenproof container and top with turkey pieces, sprinkling with brandy. Cover with the remaining mixture, then cover with a lid or piece of foil. Stand the container in a roasting tin of water. Cook at 180°C/350°F/Gas 4 for 1¼ hours. Remove the lid, cover and weight the pâté. Leave for 24 hours before serving in slices with a salad.

Note This is an excellent way of using up leftover Christmas turkey, but the terrine can, of course, be made with an individual turkey joint or rolled turkey. Use a mixture of dark and light meat from the turkey.

Turkey Terrine

Anchovy Spread

12 anchovy fillets
2 × 15ml spoons/2 tablespoons mayonnaise
3 × 15ml spoons/3 tablespoons double cream
1 slice of onion
½ × 2.5ml spoon/¼ teaspoon mustard powder
175g/6 oz full-fat soft cheese

Drain the oil from the anchovy fillets. Rinse the fillets in a little water and pat dry with kitchen paper. Blend with the mayonnaise, cream, onion and mustard powder for 10 seconds. Cut up the cheese into small cubes. With the motor running, drop the cheese through the opening in the lid, and continue blending until smooth. It may be necessary to stop the motor once or twice and push down the mixture with a spatula to ensure smooth blending.

Use on cocktail biscuits or squares of toast, or as a filling for small sandwiches.

Cheese Rarebit Spread

1 × 1 small onion
1 × 15ml spoon/1 tablespoon beer
100g/4 oz Cheddar cheese

Cut the onion into quarters and blend with the beer until the onion is finely chopped. Cut the cheese into small chunks and put through the lid of the blender with the motor running. Blend until well mixed.

Use in sandwiches or spread on toast.

Chicken Spread

4 × 15ml spoons/4 tablespoons mayonnaise
25g/1 oz chutney
1 stick of celery
1 small onion
1 × 2.5ml spoon/½ teaspoon salt
1 × 2.5ml spoon/½ teaspoon vinegar
175g/6 oz cooked chicken
2 hard-boiled eggs

Blend the mayonnaise, chutney, celery, onion, salt and vinegar until the celery and onions are coarsely chopped. Cut the chicken and eggs into pieces, and blend with the other ingredients until finely chopped.

Use as a sandwich filling.

Devilled Ham

100g/4 oz cooked ham
3 hard-boiled eggs
1 small onion
25g/1 oz chutney
1 × 15ml spoon/1 tablespoon mayonnaise
1 × 2.5ml spoon/½ teaspoon curry powder

Cut the ham, eggs and onion into pieces. Blend with the chutney, mayonnaise and curry powder to the required smoothness.

Note The mixture may be creamy, but a slightly rough texture is often more attractive, particularly if spread on toast.

Meat Paste

175g/6oz cooked meat (chicken)
50g/2oz cooked bacon, without rinds
1 × 5ml spoon/1 teaspoon French mustard
1 × 5ml spoon/1 teaspoon Worcestershire sauce
50g/2oz softened butter
pepper
garlic salt

Cut the meat and bacon into pieces. Blend with the mustard, Worcestershire sauce, butter and seasonings until creamy.

Salmon Spread

1 small onion
1 stick of celery
4 × 15ml spoons/4 tablespoons mayonnaise
a sprig of parsley
2 × 15ml spoons/2 tablespoons lemon juice
225g/8oz canned salmon
2 hard-boiled eggs
salt and pepper

Cut the onion and celery into pieces and blend with the mayonnaise, parsley and lemon juice until the vegetables are finely chopped. Drain the salmon and blend the flesh, vegetables, coarsely chopped eggs, salt and pepper until the eggs are finely chopped.

Note As canned salmon is often rather salty, do not add much salt to the blender, and adjust seasoning if necessary after blending.

Taramasalata

2 thin slices white bread (large loaf)
2 × 15ml spoons/2 tablespoons milk
2 cloves garlic
225g/8oz smoked cod's roe
150ml/¼ pint olive oil
2 × 15ml spoons/2 tablespoons lemon juice
pepper
2 × 15ml spoons/2 tablespoons double cream **or** natural yoghurt

Discard the crusts and soak the bread in the milk for 10 minutes. Blend until smooth. Blend the garlic with the cod's roe and soaked bread. With the machine running, pour in the oil slowly until the mixture looks like mayonnaise. Add the lemon juice, pepper, cream or yoghurt, and blend until just mixed. Place in a serving dish and chill for 1 hour before serving with toast.

Note The cod's roe may be fresh or from a jar. If fresh, remove the skin before processing.

Aubergine Dip

2 medium aubergines
2 lemons
100ml/4fl oz salad oil
1 × 2.5ml spoon/½ teaspoon salt
2 large cloves garlic

Split the aubergines in half lengthways. Put them, cut side down, on an ungreased baking sheet and bake at 200°C/400°F/Gas 6 for 45 minutes until the skins are crisp. Cool, then scrape the flesh from the skins. Remove the pips from the lemons and cut the flesh and rind into small pieces. Blend until very finely chopped. Add the aubergine flesh, and blend until smooth. Add the oil, salt and garlic cloves, and blend until smooth again. Serve chilled with sticks of raw vegetables.

Basic Soft Cheese Dip

175g/6oz full-fat soft cheese
salt and pepper
a little milk
flavouring (see below)

Cut the cheese into small pieces, and blend with the salt, pepper and a little milk to a dipping consistency. Add the flavouring ingredients, and blend until they are finely chopped and mixed with the cheese.

Serve chilled with potato crisps, pieces of celery, cucumber or raw carrot, or with small cocktail biscuits.

Flavourings

Anchovy
Add 50g/2oz drained anchovy fillets and 1 × 2.5ml spoon/ $\frac{1}{2}$ teaspoon lemon juice

Curry
Add 2 × 5ml spoons/2 teaspoons Worcestershire sauce, $\frac{1}{2}$ × 2.5ml spoon/$\frac{1}{4}$ teaspoon curry powder, and 50g/2oz pineapple.

Fish
Add 200g/7oz drained canned tuna or salmon and 1 × 5ml spoon/1 teaspoon Worcestershire sauce.

Crunchy
Add 50g/2oz celery, 50g/2oz apple and 50g/2oz walnuts.

Avocado Dip

1 lemon
1 large ripe avocado pear
1 small onion
4 × 15ml spoons/4 tablespoons salad oil
2 cloves garlic
salt and pepper

Peel the lemon and remove the pips. Cut in pieces and blend until very finely chopped. Cut the avocado in half, remove the stone and blend the flesh with the onion, oil, garlic and seasoning until smooth. Chill before serving with pieces of cucumber and celery, and with crisps.

Devilled Egg Dip

2 × 15ml spoons/2 tablespoons vinegar
2 × 15ml spoons/2 tablespoons mustard pickle
2 × 15ml spoons/2 tablespoons mayonnaise
50ml/2fl oz soured cream
1 small onion
salt and pepper
4 drops Tabasco sauce
2 sprigs parsley
6 hard-boiled eggs

Blend all the ingredients except the eggs until smooth. Cut the eggs in quarters and blend with the other ingredients until finely chopped. Chill before using.

Serve with crisps, carrot sticks or small cocktail sausages.

Avocado Dip, Aubergine Dip (page 51) and *Taramasalata (page 51)*

Horseradish Dip

4 × 15ml spoons/4 tablespoons soured cream
1 small onion
$\frac{1}{2}$ × 2.5ml spoon/$\frac{1}{4}$ teaspoon salt
25g/1 oz grated horseradish
2 drops Worcestershire sauce
225g/8 oz full-fat soft cheese

Blend the soured cream, coarsely chopped onion, salt, horseradish and Worcestershire sauce until the onion is finely chopped. Cut the cheese into small pieces and add to the blender slowly. Blend until smooth, and chill before using.

Serve with small hot cocktail sausages.

Pickle Dip

3 × 15ml spoons/3 tablespoons mayonnaise
2 × 15ml spoons/2 tablespoons single cream
100g/4 oz salted peanuts
a sprig of parsley
6 cocktail onions
1 × 15ml spoon/1 tablespoon tomato ketchup
1 × 15ml spoon/1 tablespoon sweet pickle

Blend all the ingredients until the nuts are finely chopped.

Serve with crisps and cocktail sausages.

PUDDINGS, DESSERTS, CAKES AND ICINGS

APPLE BUTTERSCOTCH CRUMBLE

675g/1½ lb apples
1 × 15ml spoon/1 tablespoon water
15g/½ oz butter
75g/3 oz soft brown sugar
a pinch of mixed spice

TOPPING
75g/3 oz plain flour
50g/2 oz butter
25g/1 oz soft brown sugar

Peel and core the apples and cut them in pieces. Blend until coarsely chopped, then put into an ovenproof dish with the water, butter, sugar and spice.

To make the topping, blend the flour, butter and sugar until crumbly. Put on top of the apples and press down lightly. Bake at 180°C/350°F/Gas 4 for 45 minutes.

Serve hot with cream or custard, or with melted apricot jam.

SWEET SOUFFLÉS

50g/2 oz plain flour
300ml/½ pint milk
3 size 1–2 eggs, separated
75g/3 oz butter
50g/2 oz caster sugar
flavourings (see below)

Blend the flour, milk and egg yolks on low speed until smooth. Melt the butter and stir in the milk mixture and sugar, cooking gently and stirring well until smooth and thick. Remove from the heat. Whisk the egg whites to stiff peaks and fold into the sauce. Grease a 1.2 litre/2 pint soufflé dish, fill with the mixture and bake at 190°C/375°F/Gas 5 for 45 minutes. Serve at once.

Note This method of cooking gives a crisp crust. For a softer soufflé, bake the dish in a pan of hot but not boiling water in the oven.

Flavourings

Apple
Add 4 × 15ml spoons/4 tablespoons sweet cooked apples and a squeeze of lemon juice to the cooked sauce, blend for 10 seconds, and fold in the egg whites.

Apricot
Add 6 canned apricot halves to the cooked sauce and blend for 10 seconds before folding in the egg whites.

Chocolate
Blend 50g/2 oz plain chocolate with the milk mixture before cooking the sauce.

Lemon
Add the grated rind and juice of 1 lemon to the sauce before folding in the egg whites.

Liqueur
Stir in 5 × 15ml spoons/5 tablespoons Cointreau or Grand Marnier just before folding in the egg whites.

Soft Fruit
Add 150ml/¼ pint sieved raspberries or strawberries to the cooked sauce and blend for 10 seconds before folding in the egg whites.

French Fritters with Cherry Sauce

100g/4 oz plain flour
a pinch of salt
2 × 5ml spoons/2 teaspoons icing sugar
8 × 15ml spoons/8 tablespoons water
2 × 15ml spoons/2 tablespoons oil
2 egg whites
25g/1 oz caster sugar
1 × 2.5ml spoon/$\frac{1}{2}$ teaspoon ground cinnamon
450g/1 lb canned black cherries
15g/$\frac{1}{2}$ oz cornflour

Blend the flour, salt, icing sugar, water and oil until creamy and smooth. Whisk the egg whites to stiff peaks and fold in the batter. Heat about 2.5cm/1 inch oil in a frying pan, and fry teaspoonfuls of the mixture for about 3 minutes, turning once, until light and golden. Drain on absorbent paper and toss in a mixture of caster sugar and cinnamon.

Drain the juice from the cherries into a pan and mix a little juice with the cornflour. Add to the remaining juice and bring to the boil, stirring until thick and smooth. Add the cherries, and heat through. Pour the sauce over the fritters.

Fruit Pancakes

300ml/$\frac{1}{2}$ pint milk
1 size 1–2 egg
1 × 2.5ml spoon/$\frac{1}{2}$ teaspoon salt
100g/4 oz plain flour
2 eating apples
100g/4 oz raisins
50g/2 oz soft brown sugar
2 × 15ml spoons/2 tablespoons water
icing **or** caster sugar

Blend the milk, egg and salt until mixed. Add the flour, and blend until smooth and creamy. Pour sufficient batter into a frying pan to cover the base, and make a thin pancake. Continue with the rest of the batter. Peel and core the apples, cut in pieces, and blend until finely chopped. Simmer with the raisins, sugar and water until the apples are just soft. Fill the pancakes with the fruit mixture and fold over.

Serve with a sprinkling of icing or caster sugar, and with cream or Butterscotch Sauce (page 74).

Fruit Pancakes with Butterscotch Sauce

Lemon Crumb Pudding

2.5cm/1 inch thick slice bread
4 eggs, separated
2 × 15ml spoons/2 tablespoons lemon juice
225g/8 oz sugar
50g/2 oz softened butter

Break the bread into pieces and make into breadcrumbs in the blender. Put the crumbs into a bowl. Blend the yolks, lemon juice, sugar and butter for 20 seconds, then stir into the crumbs. Whisk the egg whites to stiff peaks, and fold into the crumb mixture. Put into a greased pie dish, and bake at 180°C/350°F/Gas 4 for 45 minutes. Serve hot with cream.

Queen of Puddings

6 × 2.5cm/1 inch thick slices bread
450ml/$\frac{3}{4}$ pint milk
50g/2 oz sugar
1 thin strip of lemon rind
50g/2 oz butter
2 eggs, separated
25g/1 oz strawberry jam
25g/1 oz caster sugar

Break the bread into small pieces and make into breadcrumbs in the blender. Put the crumbs in a bowl. Warm the milk without boiling, and blend with the sugar, lemon rind, butter and egg yolks for 10 seconds. Pour over the crumbs, stir well, and put into a greased pie dish. Bake at 160°C/325°F/Gas 3 for 30 minutes. Spread the jam on top of the pudding. Whisk the egg whites to soft peaks. Gradually beat in the caster sugar until the mixture is stiff and glossy. Spread on top of the jam, and continue baking for 15 minutes.

Raisin Pudding

4 × 2.5cm/1 inch thick slices bread
100g/4 oz seedless raisins
450ml/$\frac{3}{4}$ pint milk
grated rind of $\frac{1}{2}$ orange
2 eggs
65g/2$\frac{1}{2}$ oz sugar
50g/2 oz softened butter
a pinch of salt

Break the bread into pieces and make into breadcrumbs in the blender. Put into a bowl, and mix with the raisins. Blend the milk, orange rind, eggs, sugar, butter and salt for 20 seconds. Pour on to the crumbs and raisins, and put the mixture into a greased pie dish. Put the dish into a roasting tin with water, and bake at 180°C/350°F/Gas 4 for 1 hour. Serve hot with cream.

Baked Coconut Pudding

100g/4 oz white bread
75g/3 oz desiccated coconut
600ml/1 pint milk
1 egg
25g/1 oz butter
100g/4 oz sugar
grated rind of $\frac{1}{2}$ lemon
50g/2 oz jam

Break the bread in pieces and make into breadcrumbs in the blender. Mix with the coconut. Bring the milk to the boil, cool slightly and blend with the egg, butter, sugar and lemon rind for 10 seconds. Add the bread and coconut, and blend on medium speed until well mixed. Spread the jam in the bottom of a greased ovenproof dish, put in the coconut mixture and bake at 180°C/350°F/Gas 4 for 40 minutes. Serve with custard.

Apple Popovers

15g/½ oz cooking fat
2 medium cooking apples
25g/1 oz caster sugar
juice of 1 lemon
25g/1 oz soft brown sugar

BATTER
300ml/½ pint milk
1 egg
1 × 2.5ml spoon/½ teaspoon salt
100g/4 oz plain flour
grated rind of 1 lemon

Divide the fat between six 10cm/4 inch patty tins and heat at 220°C/425°F/Gas 7 until the fat is very hot. Peel, core and slice the apples. Toss in the caster sugar and divide between the tins.

To make the batter, blend the milk, egg, salt and flour until creamy, adding the flour and lemon rind last.

Pour the batter over the apples and bake for 30 minutes. Just before serving, put the juice of the lemon and the brown sugar into a saucepan, bring to the boil and boil for 2 minutes until syrupy. Serve spooned into the centres of the popovers.

Apple Crunch

450g/1 lb cooking apples
sugar
100g/4 oz brown bread
50g/2 oz butter
50g/2 oz Demerara sugar

DECORATION
150ml/¼ pint double cream
50g/2 oz plain chocolate

Peel, core and slice the apples. Put into a pan with just enough water to cover, and simmer until soft. Cool and sweeten to taste. Break the bread into pieces and make into breadcrumbs in the blender. Melt the butter in a pan, and add the breadcrumbs and Demerara sugar mixed together. Fry gently until golden-brown. Cool completely.

Arrange alternate layers of apple and bread mixture in a glass serving dish, finishing with a layer of breadcrumbs. Chill in a refrigerator. Whip the cream until stiff and spread on top of the crumbs. Blend the chocolate until grated, and sprinkle over the cream.

Apple Flummery

75g/3 oz pearl barley
1.2litres/2 pints water
675g/$1\frac{1}{2}$ lb eating apples
50g/2 oz caster sugar
juice of 1 lemon
4 × 15ml spoons/4 tablespoons single cream

Put the barley into the water and bring to the boil. Peel, core and slice the apples. Add to the barley and simmer until both the apples and barley are soft. Cool slightly, and blend until smooth and creamy. Return to the pan and add the sugar and lemon juice. Bring to the boil, then cool and stir in the cream. Chill before serving.

Blackcurrant Flummery

450g/1 lb blackcurrants
600ml/1 pint water
15g/$\frac{1}{2}$ oz cornflour
100g/4 oz caster sugar
2 × 5ml spoons/2 teaspoons lemon juice
2 eggs, separated

Put the currants into the water and simmer until the fruit is soft. Blend the fruit and liquid, then sieve. Mix the cornflour with a little of the purée, then add to the remaining blackcurrant purée. Bring to the boil, add the sugar and lemon juice, and cook for 2 minutes, stirring all the time. Leave to cool, then blend with the egg yolks until smooth and creamy. Whisk the egg whites to stiff peaks and fold into the blackcurrant mixture. Chill before serving with cream.

Apricot Whip

450g/1 lb canned apricots in syrup
50g/2 oz orange marmalade
50g/2 oz blanched almonds

Blend the apricots and syrup with the marmalade until smooth, then pour into a serving dish. Spread the almonds on a baking sheet and bake at 180°C/350°F/Gas 4 for 5 minutes until golden-brown. If the oven is in use for any other purpose, the almonds can be browned under the grill. Scatter the almonds over the apricot whip, and chill before serving with cream.

Instant Banana Mousse

6 bananas
1 × 15ml spoon/1 tablespoon lemon juice
2 egg whites
100g/4 oz caster sugar
redcurrant jelly

Cut up the bananas and blend with the lemon juice until smooth and creamy. Whisk the egg whites to stiff peaks and slowly add the caster sugar, whisking until it is completely mixed with the egg whites. Pour in the banana pureé and whisk until just mixed. Put into individual bowls and serve at once with cream. Top each portion with a spoonful of sharp jelly such as redcurrant.

Variation

Honey may be substituted for half the sugar and should be blended with the bananas.

Fruit Mousse

350g/12 oz fruit (see Method)
sugar
25g/1 oz gelatine
1 × 15ml spoon/1 tablespoon lemon juice
2 eggs, separated

The fruit may be fresh, canned or frozen. If the fresh or frozen fruit is juicy (eg raspberries), no further liquid will be required. Fresh fruit should be cooked in a little water until just soft. Sweeten the fruit lightly to taste. Put the gelatine into 2 × 15ml spoons/2 tablespoons water, and stand the bowl in hot water until the gelatine melts and is syrupy. Blend the fruit for 1 minute with a little cooking liquid, or syrup from the can and the gelatine, lemon juice and egg yolks. Put into a bowl and leave in a cool place until nearly set. Whisk the egg whites until stiff, and gently fold into the fruit mixture.

Marmalade Cream

450g/1 lb cottage cheese
2 × 15ml spoons/2 tablespoons marmalade
2 × 15ml spoons/2 tablespoons caster sugar
2 × 15ml spoons/2 tablespoons brandy **or** whisky
1 × 15ml spoon/1 tablespoon lemon juice

DECORATION
grated rind of 1 orange

Blend all the ingredients first on low speed, scraping down if necessary. When well mixed, increase to high speed and blend for 10 seconds. Put into six individual dishes and chill for 4 hours before serving. Just before serving, sprinkle with grated orange rind.

Serve with crisp shortbread.

Lemon Flummery

300ml/½ pint water
25g/1 oz butter
grated rind and juice of 1 lemon
25g/1 oz plain flour
100g/4 oz caster sugar
1 size 1–2 egg, separated
4 digestive biscuits

Put the water into a pan with the butter and grated lemon rind, and bring to the boil. Remove from the heat and cool slightly. Blend the juice of the lemon, the flour and sugar and the liquid for 30 seconds. Add the egg yolk and blend for 5 seconds. Put the mixture into a saucepan and bring slowly to the boil, stirring gently. Simmer for 10 minutes and pour into a bowl. Whisk the egg white until stiff, and fold into the lemon mixture. Chill until cold and firm. Break up the biscuits and make into coarse crumbs in the blender. Sprinkle on top of the flummery, and serve with cream.

Raspberry Foam

450g/1 lb raspberries
75g/3 oz caster sugar
300ml/½ pint double cream
2 egg whites

Put the raspberries into a bowl with the sugar and leave for 1 hour to draw out the juices. Blend on high speed, then sieve. Blend the raspberry purée and cream on low speed until well mixed. Whisk the egg whites to stiff peaks and fold into the raspberry cream. Chill before serving with small sweet biscuits.

Apple Snow

675g/$1\frac{1}{2}$ lb cooking apples (see **Note**)
1 × 5ml spoon/1 teaspoon grated lemon rind
1 × 5ml spoon/1 teaspoon lemon juice
2 × 15ml spoons/2 tablespoons water
50g/2 oz caster sugar
2 egg whites
150ml/$\frac{1}{4}$ pint double cream

Peel, core and slice the apples. Put into a saucepan with the lemon rind, juice and water, and cook until the apples are soft. Blend with the sugar until smooth, then cool. Whisk the egg whites to stiff peaks. Fold in the apples in small quantities until well mixed in. Whip the cream lightly, and fold into the apple mixture. Chill before serving.

Note Use cooking apples which become fluffy when cooked.
If liked, this mixture may be frozen as ice cream, beating once during freezing.

Date Whip

225g/8 oz pitted dates (see **Note**)
100ml/4 fl oz orange juice
1 × 5ml spoon/1 teaspoon lemon juice
100g/4 oz walnut halves

Cut the dates into pieces and simmer with the orange juice for 10 minutes. Blend for 30 seconds. Add the lemon juice and walnuts, and blend for 10 seconds until the nuts are finely chopped. Spoon into individual dishes and chill before serving.

Note Block dates are the easiest and cheapest to use for this recipe.

Jelly Whip

150ml/$\frac{1}{4}$ pint water
1 × 600ml/1 pint pkt fruit jelly
1 × 170g/6 oz can evaporated milk

Boil the water in a small saucepan, reduce the heat and put in the jelly, broken into pieces. Simmer until the jelly has melted. Blend the evaporated milk until light and fluffy. With the blender running, slowly pour in the liquid jelly and continue blending until well mixed. Pour into a bowl and chill.

Bakewell Pudding

175g/6 oz prepared shortcrust pastry
50g/2 oz strawberry jam
4 eggs
4 drops almond essence
100g/4 oz caster sugar
75g/3 oz blanched almonds
100g/4 oz softened butter
1 thin strip of lemon rind

Line a 17.5cm/7 inch pie plate with the pastry, and spread with the jam. Blend all the other ingredients for 30 seconds until well mixed. Pour into the pastry case. Bake at 220°C/425°F/Gas 7 for 25 minutes until golden-brown. Serve hot or cold.

Baked Cheesecake

50g/2 oz digestive biscuits
450g/1 lb cottage cheese
1 × 5ml spoon/1 teaspoon lemon juice
1 × 5ml spoon/1 teaspoon grated orange rind
1 × 15ml spoon/1 tablespoon cornflour
2 eggs, separated
2 × 15ml spoons/2 tablespoons double cream
100g/4 oz caster sugar

Grease the sides of a 20cm/8 inch cake tin with a removable base, and line the base with greased paper. Break up the biscuits and make into crumbs in the blender. Sprinkle into the base of the tin. Blend the cottage cheese, lemon juice, orange rind, cornflour, egg yolks and double cream until smooth. Whisk the egg whites to stiff peaks. Beat in half the sugar, and then fold in the rest. Fold into the cottage cheese mixture, then put into the prepared tin. Bake at 180°C/350°F/Gas 4 for 1 hour. Turn off the oven and leave the cheesecake until cold. Remove from the tin and eat with fresh, frozen or canned fruit.

Jelly Chiffon Pie

225g/8 oz prepared shortcrust pastry
1 × 142g/5 oz packet jelly (see **Note**)
150ml/$\frac{1}{4}$ pint boiling water
2 eggs, separated
75g/3 oz caster sugar
150ml/$\frac{1}{4}$ pint double cream

DECORATION
fruit **or** nuts

Roll out the pastry and use to line a 20cm/8 inch flan ring. Bake blind at 220°C/420°F/Gas 7 for 15 minutes, then continue baking for 15 minutes until crisp and golden. Leave until cold.

Put the jelly and water into a heavy saucepan and heat gently until the jelly melts. Remove from the heat, and cool until just beginning to thicken. Blend with the egg yolks and sugar until smooth and creamy. Whisk the egg whites to stiff peaks and fold in the jelly mixture. Pour into the pastry case, and chill. Just before serving, whip the cream until stiff, and pile into the centre of the pie. Decorate with fruit or nuts.

Note Use a strongly flavoured jelly such as orange, raspberry or blackcurrant.

Basic Ice Cream

450ml/¾ pint creamy milk
1 vanilla pod
2 size 1–2 egg yolks
50g/2 oz sugar
a pinch of salt
150ml/¼ pint double cream

Warm the milk with the vanilla pod just to boiling point. Remove the pod, and blend the milk with the egg yolks, sugar and salt for 10 seconds. Cook the mixture in a double saucepan (or in a bowl over a pan of hot water) until the custard is of a coating consistency. Leave to cool. Whip the cream lightly and fold into the cooled custard. Pour into a freezer tray and freeze at the lowest setting for 1 hour, then blend again for 10 seconds. Scrape down if necessary and continue blending until the mixture is just smooth. Freeze for 1 hour, then repeat the blending, and freeze for a further hour. This will give a really smooth ice cream.

Variations

1) Scald 25g/1 oz ground coffee in warm milk, and strain before blending.
2) Melt 50g/2 oz plain chocolate in 4 × 15ml spoons/4 tablespoons hot water, and add to the milk before blending.

Biscuit Tortoni

50g/2 oz toasted blanched almonds
2 × 15ml spoons/2 tablespoons water
65g/2½ oz caster sugar
2 × 15ml spoons/2 tablespoons sherry
3 egg yolks
250ml/8fl oz double cream

Blend the nuts until coarsely ground. Put into a bowl. Put the water and sugar into a small pan, bring to the boil, and boil for 3 minutes. Blend the sherry and egg yolks at high speed, gradually pouring in the hot syrup. Whip the cream to soft peaks, and then fold in the blended mixture. Put into four serving dishes which will resist a low temperature and sprinkle with the ground nuts. Put in a freezer for 2 hours before serving.

Raspberry Water Ice

100g/4 oz sugar
300ml/½ pint water
450g/1 lb raspberries
1 egg white (optional)

Put the sugar and water in a saucepan, bring to the boil, boil for 5 minutes, and then cool. Blend the raspberries and sieve them. Blend with the sugar syrup for 15 seconds. Pour into a freezer tray and freeze for 3 hours. Half-way through freezing, blend the mixture again. For a lighter ice, fold in a stiffly whisked egg white at this stage.

Variation

The same method can be used for blackberries, strawberries or blackcurrants, but blackcurrants need to be cooked in a little water before blending.

Fruit Mousse (page 61) and *Raspberry Water Ice*

Banana Bread

3 ripe bananas
225g/8 oz plain flour
3 × 5ml spoons/3 teaspoons baking powder
a pinch of salt
50g/2 oz soft margarine
50g/2 oz light soft brown sugar
grated rind of 1 lemon
1 egg
3–4 × 15ml spoons/3–4 tablespoons milk

Cut the bananas into pieces. Blend until puréed, then put to one side. Add all the other ingredients gradually through the hole in the lid with the machine running, until a soft batter is formed. If necessary, add a little more milk. Put the mixture into a 450g/1 lb greased and floured loaf tin, and bake at 190°C/375°F/Gas 5 for 45 minutes. Turn out and cool on a wire rack. Serve sliced and buttered.

Chocolate Crumb Cake

225g/8 oz sweet biscuits
100g/4 oz butter
25g/1 oz sugar
25g/1 oz cocoa
1 × 15ml spoon/1 tablespoon golden syrup
100g/4 oz plain chocolate

Break up the biscuits and blend a few at a time to make fine crumbs. Melt the butter with the sugar, cocoa and syrup until just liquid. Mix in the crumbs and press into a greased 17.5cm/7 inch square tin about 2.5cm/1 inch deep. Melt the chocolate over hot water and pour on top of the cake. Chill for 5 hours, then cut into squares to serve.

Morning Cake

1 egg
75ml/3fl oz milk
40g/1½ oz melted butter
½ × 2.5ml spoon/¼ teaspoon lemon essence
1 × 2.5ml spoon/½ teaspoon vanilla essence
100g/4 oz caster sugar
125g/5 oz plain flour
1 × 5ml spoon/1 teaspoon baking powder
a pinch of salt

Blend the egg, milk, melted butter and essences until smooth. Add the sugar and blend for 5 seconds. Sift the flour, baking powder and salt, and blend with the other ingredients for 10 seconds. Pour into a greased rectangular tin (about 25 × 17.5cm/10 × 7 inches) and bake at 180°C/350°F/Gas 4 for 25 minutes. Cut into squares and serve warm.

Variation

Cover the surface of the batter closely with stoned fresh plums or cooked prunes, or a thick layer of thinly sliced apples. Sprinkle with 50g/2 oz sugar and a pinch of cinnamon before baking. This can be served as a cake, or as a dessert with cream or custard.

Walnut Loaf

350g/12 oz plain flour
2 × 5ml spoons/2 teaspoons baking powder
a pinch of salt
225g/8 oz sugar
2 eggs
300ml/½ pint milk
40g/1½ oz melted butter
100g/4 oz walnut halves

Sift together the flour, baking powder and salt into a bowl. Blend the sugar, eggs, milk and butter at high speed until well mixed. Add the walnut halves, and blend on low speed until finely chopped. Pour on to the flour mixture, and fold in. Put into a greased 900g/2 lb loaf tin and leave to stand for 20 minutes. Bake at 180°C/350°F/Gas 4 for 1¼ hours. Cool, slice and spread with butter and honey.

Cottage Cheese Drop Scones

50g/2 oz self-raising flour
25g/1 oz melted butter
100g/4 oz cottage cheese
2 eggs
1 × 15ml spoon/1 tablespoon milk

Sift the flour into a bowl. Blend the butter, cottage cheese, eggs and milk until well mixed. Add the flour and blend until creamy. Cook in spoonfuls on a hot greased griddle or thick frying pan until golden. Serve freshly cooked with bacon, jam or syrup.

Potato Pancakes

450g/1 lb potatoes
1 small onion
2 eggs
50g/2 oz plain flour
1 × 5ml spoon/1 teaspoon salt
½ × 2.5ml spoon/¼ teaspoon baking powder

Cut the potatoes into small pieces, and dry well with kitchen paper. Cut in pieces. Blend all the ingredients until finely chopped. Stop the motor and scrape down the potatoes with a spatula if necessary. Pour this batter on to a hot greased griddle or thick frying pan, and brown on each side. Serve hot with butter.

Note Potato pancakes can also be used as an accompaniment to bacon or sausages.

Coventry Tarts

225g/8 oz prepared shortcrust pastry
225g/8 oz cottage cheese
100g/4 oz caster sugar
a pinch of salt
a pinch of ground nutmeg
1 × 15ml spoon/1 tablespoon orange juice
50g/2 oz melted butter
1 egg

DECORATION
4 × 15ml spoons/4 tablespoons apple, redcurrant **or** cranberry jelly

Roll out the pastry to line 16 tartlet tins. Blend the rest of the ingredients on low speed until smooth and creamy. Fill the pastry cases two-thirds full with the mixture. Bake at 190°C/375°F/Gas 5 for 20 minutes until the pastry is golden and the filling is set and lightly coloured. Serve freshly baked with a spoonful of jelly on each one.

Drop Scones

225g/8 oz plain flour
a pinch of salt
1 × 5ml spoon/1 teaspoon bicarbonate of soda
2 × 5ml spoons/2 teaspoons cream of tartar
50g/2 oz sugar
2 eggs
150ml/$\frac{1}{4}$ pint milk
25g/1 oz softened butter

Sift together the flour, salt, bicarbonate of soda and cream of tartar, and stir in the sugar. Blend the eggs, milk and butter until smooth. Add the flour mixture, and blend until thick and creamy. Cook in spoonfuls on a hot greased griddle or thick frying pan until both sides are golden. When cooked, put on a wire rack and wrap in a clean cloth to keep soft. Serve spread with butter.

Variation

Put 3 thin slices of banana on each scone while cooking and before turning over. Serve with butter and sugar, or with syrup.

Butter Icing

2 × 15ml spoons/2 tablespoons liquid (see **Note**)
100g/4 oz softened butter
175g/6 oz icing sugar
flavourings (see below)

Blend all the ingredients until smooth and light.

Note The liquid may be fruit juice, thin cream or strong coffee.

Flavourings

Chocolate
Add 15g/$\frac{1}{2}$ oz cocoa or 50g/2 oz melted plain chocolate.
Coffee
Add 2 × 5ml spoons/2 teaspoons coffee essence.
Lemon
Add 1 × 5ml spoon/1 teaspoon lemon juice and 1 × 5ml spoon/1 teaspoon grated lemon rind (or a few drops of lemon essence).
Mocha
Add 15g/$\frac{1}{2}$ oz cocoa and a few drops of coffee essence.
Orange
Add 2 × 5ml spoons/2 teaspoons orange juice and 1 × 5ml spoon/1 teaspoon grated orange rind (or a few drops of orange essence).
Vanilla
Add a few drops vanilla essence.

Drop Scones and *Walnut Loaf (page 67)*

GALE'S
HONEY

Confectioner's Custard

50g/2 oz sugar
2 egg yolks
a few drops vanilla essence
300ml/½ pint milk
25g/1 oz plain flour
15g/½ oz butter

Blend the sugar, egg yolks, essence, milk and flour for 30 seconds until creamy. Put into a heavy saucepan and cook gently, stirring well until thick. Stir in the butter, and leave to cool.

Use for filling cakes, choux pastry and the bases of fruit flans.

Cream Cheese Icing

175g/6 oz cream cheese
50ml/2fl oz double cream
1 × 2.5ml spoon/½ teaspoon vanilla **or** lemon essence
25g/1 oz soft butter
400g/14 oz icing sugar

Cut the cream cheese into small pieces. Blend with the cream, essence and butter for 15 seconds. Add one-third of the sugar, and blend for 30 seconds. While the motor is running, add the remaining sugar through the hole in the lid, and blend until smooth.

Note This gives enough icing to fill and top a 17.5cm/7 inch cake.

Mocha Fudge Icing

175g/6 oz plain chocolate
40g/1½ oz soft butter
1 egg
1 × 5ml spoon/1 teaspoon vanilla essence
75g/3 oz icing sugar
150ml/¼ pint hot strong black coffee

Cut the chocolate in pieces and blend until finely chopped. Blend all the ingredients except the coffee for 5 seconds. Pour in the hot coffee and blend for 15 seconds.

Note This gives a very creamy texture, but more icing sugar can be added slowly to give a firmer icing.

Royal Icing

1 egg white
1 × 5ml spoon/1 teaspoon lemon juice
115g/4½ oz icing sugar

Blend all the ingredients until smooth. Use at once for piping.

Note This icing is not stiff enough to cover a cake, as a blender cannot cope with the amount of icing sugar necessary for a very firm texture.

Preserves and Pickles

Cranberry Relish

450g/1 lb cranberries
1 orange
75ml/3 fl oz boiling water
100g/4 oz seedless raisins
675g/1½ lb sugar
225g/8 oz walnuts

Put the cranberries into 150ml/¼ pint cold water and boil until the skins break. Blend for 5 seconds. Peel the orange and cut the flesh in small pieces. Add to the blender, and blend for 5 seconds. Add the cranberry and orange mixture to the boiling water, raisins and sugar. Bring to the boil and simmer for 20 minutes. Blend the walnuts until coarsely chopped. Stir into the cranberry mixture, cool, then fill small jars, seal and label.

Note This can be eaten with turkey, pork or ham, and it is also very good as a filling for small tarts.

Date Chutney

450g/1 lb stoned block dates
100g/4 oz onions
300ml/½ pint water
100g/4 oz seedless raisins
15g/½ oz garlic
6 chillies
100g/4 oz sugar
1 × 5ml spoon/1 teaspoon salt
600ml/1 pint vinegar

Cut the dates and onions in pieces and blend with some of the water until well chopped. Put into a saucepan with the raisins and remaining water. Crush the garlic and the chillies. Put into a piece of muslin or thin cotton and tie into a bag before hanging from the handle of the saucepan. Simmer the onion mixture until the onions are tender. Add the sugar, salt and vinegar, and simmer for 30 minutes, stirring until thick and brown. Remove the bag of garlic and chillies. Blend the chutney for 30 seconds, then pour into warm jars, seal and label.

PEAR CHUTNEY

1.8kg/4 lb ripe eating pears
grated rind and juice of 2 oranges
675g/1½ lb sugar
1 × 5ml spoon/1 teaspoon ground cloves
1 × 5ml spoon/1 teaspoon ground cinnamon
1 × 5ml spoon/1 teaspoon ground allspice
600ml/1 pint vinegar
350g/12 oz seedless raisins

Peel and core the pears, and cut the flesh into pieces. Blend on low speed until chopped. Put all the ingredients into a saucepan and bring to the boil. Simmer for 2 hours, stirring frequently, until thick and brown. Pour into warm jars, seal and label.

PLUM CHUTNEY

900g/2 lb stoned plums
450g/1 lb carrots
600ml/1 pint vinegar
450g/1 lb seedless raisins
450g/1 lb soft brown sugar
1 clove garlic
25g/1 oz chillies
25g/1 oz ground ginger
40g/1½ oz salt

Blend the plums on low speed until chopped, then put into a saucepan. Cut the carrots into pieces, then blend with some of the vinegar until finely chopped. Put into the saucepan with the rest of the vinegar, the raisins and sugar. Crush the garlic clove, and chop the chillies. Add to the saucepan with the ginger and salt. Bring to the boil, and simmer until thick and brown, stirring well. Pour into warm jars, seal and label.

RED TOMATO CHUTNEY

450g/1 lb ripe tomatoes
100g/4 oz apples
225g/8 oz onions
450g/1 lb seedless raisins
300ml/½ pint vinegar
100g/4 oz soft brown sugar
1 × 5ml spoon/1 teaspoon salt
1 × 5ml spoon/1 teaspoon ground ginger
a pinch of Cayenne pepper

Skin the tomatoes and remove the pips. Peel and core the apples and cut the flesh into pieces. Cut the onions into pieces and blend with the tomatoes, apples and raisins and a little of the vinegar until finely chopped. Put all the ingredients into a saucepan, bring to the boil and simmer for 1 hour until thick and brown. Stir well, pour into warm jars, seal and label.

GOOSEBERRY CHUTNEY

1.4kg/3 lb gooseberries
300ml/½ pint vinegar
550g/1¼ lb sugar
15g/½ oz ground cloves

Top and tail the gooseberries and blend them with some of the vinegar until chopped in small pieces. Put all the ingredients into a saucepan, bring to the boil, and simmer for 45 minutes, stirring until brown and thick. Pour into warm jars, seal and label.

Apple Butter

450g/1lb cooking apples (see **Note**)
150ml/¼ pint water
225g/8 oz caster sugar
1 × 5ml spoon/1 teaspoon ground cinnamon
½ × 2.5ml spoon/¼ teaspoon ground allspice
1 × 2.5ml spoon/½ teaspoon ground nutmeg
½ × 2.5ml spoon/¼ teaspoon ground cloves
a pinch of salt
1 thin slice of lemon

Cut the apples into quarters, but do not peel them. Remove the cores, and cut the flesh into pieces. Blend all the ingredients until the apples are finely chopped. Cook gently for 45 minutes, stirring occasionally, then pour into hot jars, cover at once, and label.

This makes a good filling for tarts, but fruit butters used to be stored in wide-topped jars. They were then turned out, cut into slices, and served with cream.

Note Use apples which become fluffy when cooked.

Variation

Substitute plums or damsons for apples.

Pepper and Onion Pickle

8 green peppers
3 large onions
100g/4 oz sugar
350ml/12 fl oz vinegar
15g/½ oz salt

Cut the peppers in quarters and remove the stems, membranes and seeds. Cut the onions in pieces. Blend the peppers and onions in small quantities with just enough water to cover until the vegetables are chopped in small pieces. Drain off the water and put the peppers and onions into a bowl. Cover with boiling water and leave for 15 minutes. Drain and cover again with boiling water, and leave for a further 15 minutes. Drain again and put into a large saucepan with the sugar, vinegar and salt. Bring to the boil and simmer for 30 minutes. Pack into hot jars, seal and label.

Use as a pickle, or add a few spoonfuls to winter casseroles or pies when peppers are expensive.

Sweet Sauces and Drinks

Butterscotch Sauce

250ml/8fl oz evaporated milk
100g/4 oz soft brown sugar
100g/4 oz caster sugar
50g/2 oz softened butter
1 × 15ml spoon/1 tablespoon liquid honey
1 × 2.5ml spoon/½ teaspoon vanilla essence
a pinch of salt

Blend all the ingredients until smooth. Store in a refrigerator. Serve hot or cold.

Chocolate Sauce

100g/4 oz plain chocolate
225g/8 oz sugar
150ml/¼ pint hot black coffee **or** milk
a pinch of salt
1 × 2.5ml spoon/½ teaspoon vanilla essence

Blend the chocolate until finely chopped, then blend with all the ingredients until smooth. Cool and store in a covered jar in a refrigerator.

Chocolate Fudge Sauce

15g/½ oz butter
2 × 15ml spoons/2 tablespoons milk
1 × 15ml spoon/1 tablespoon golden syrup
25g/1 oz plain chocolate
100g/4 oz soft brown sugar
1 × 2.5ml spoon/½ teaspoon vanilla essence

Warm the butter, milk and syrup and blend until smooth with the chocolate. Stir over low heat with the sugar until the sugar has dissolved. Bring to the boil and boil steadily without stirring for 5 minutes. Remove from the heat and stir in the vanilla essence.

Serve hot over ice cream or steamed or baked puddings.

Custard Sauce

600ml/1 pint milk
25g/1 oz cornflour
1 egg
25g/1 oz butter
50g/2 oz sugar
1 × 2.5ml spoon/½ teaspoon vanilla essence

Mix a little of the milk with the cornflour. Bring the remaining milk to the boil. Pour on to the cornflour and return to the saucepan to cook for a minute, stirring all the time. Remove from the heat. Blend the egg, butter, sugar and essence on medium speed, pouring the milk through the centre of the blender cap.

Serve hot on puddings or pies, or cold with fruit.

Lemon Sauce

1 lemon
25g/1 oz soft butter
300ml/½ pint water
25g/1 oz cornflour
25g/1 oz sugar

Cut up the lemon and remove the pips. Blend with all the other ingredients on high speed for 10 seconds. Strain into a pan and bring to the boil, stirring well. Continue cooking for 3 minutes until smooth and creamy.

Serve hot over steamed or baked puddings.

Raspberry Sauce

225g/8 oz raspberries
50g/2 oz icing sugar

Blend the fruit and sugar to a thick purée, adding a little water if too thick. Put through a sieve, and chill.

Rum Sauce

300ml/½ pint milk
25g/1 oz cornflour
15g/½ oz sugar
15g/½ oz unsalted butter
1 × 15ml spoon/1 tablespoon rum

Blend the milk and cornflour until smooth. Put into a saucepan with the sugar and bring to the boil, stirring well. Simmer for 3 minutes, then add the butter and rum, and blend until creamy. Serve hot.

Banana Flip

2 bananas
300ml/½ pint milk
100g/4 oz cottage cheese
15g/½ oz soft brown sugar

Cut the bananas into pieces and blend with the milk for 30 seconds. Add the cottage cheese and sugar, and blend again for 15 seconds. Serve cold.

Note This is enough for 2 servings.

Egg Nog

3 eggs
300ml/½ pint milk
50g/2 oz sugar
150ml/¼ pint brandy, rum, whisky **or** sherry
300ml/½ pint single cream
3 ice cubes, crushed

Blend all the ingredients for 10 seconds.

Variation

A warm drink may be made by omitting the ice, and warming the milk and cream. Add them slowly through the opening in the blender lid until the mixture is creamy, and sprinkle nutmeg on each serving.

Note This is enough for 4 servings.

Fresh Fruit Shake for Slimmers

4 ice cubes
175g/6 oz strawberries, raspberries, peaches, apricots **or** bananas
600ml/1 pint skimmed milk
artificial sweetener

Wrap the ice cubes in a tea-towel, and break each cube with a hammer or rolling-pin. Blend with all the ingredients for 1 minute until smooth.

Note This is enough for 3 servings.

Hawaiian Punch

2 slices fresh **or** canned pineapple
1 medium orange
1 banana
450ml/¾ pint water
ice cubes **or** crushed ice

Cut the pineapple into chunks. Peel the orange, remove the pips, and cut the flesh into quarters. Cut the banana into pieces. Blend all the ingredients for 30 seconds. Put the ice cubes or crushed ice into glasses, and pour over the punch.

Note This is enough for 4 servings.

Honey Lemonade

4 lemons
75g/3 oz liquid honey

Peel the lemons and remove the pips. Cut the flesh into pieces and blend for 30 seconds. Add the honey, and blend until the honey is incorporated. Store in a refrigerator, and dilute with water to serve.

Note About 3 × 15ml spoons/3 tablespoons of concentrate to 300ml/½ pint water will be the right proportion.

Vegetable Health Drink (page 79), Hawaiian Punch, Mexican Chocolate (page 78) and Lemon Cordial (page 78)

Ice Cream Soda

2 ice cubes
50g/2 oz raspberries **or** strawberries
15g/$\frac{1}{2}$ oz sugar
50g/2 oz vanilla ice cream
150ml/$\frac{1}{4}$ pint soda water

Wrap the ice cubes in a tea-towel, and break each cube into four or five pieces with a hammer or rolling-pin. Blend with the fruit, sugar and ice cream until smooth. Strain into a tall glass, and add the soda water.

Note This is enough for 1 serving.

Lemon Cordial

1 thin-skinned lemon
50g/2 oz sugar
6 ice cubes, crushed
750ml/1$\frac{1}{4}$ pints water

DECORATION
mint leaves

Do not peel the lemon, but cut it into pieces. Blend with the other ingredients for 10 seconds. Strain and pour into tall glasses. Decorate with a few fresh mint leaves.

Note This is enough for 3 servings.

Meal-in-a-Glass

1 egg
300ml/$\frac{1}{2}$ pint orange juice
1 × 15ml spoon/1 tablespoon liquid honey
1 × 15ml spoon/1 tablespoon lemon juice
15g/$\frac{1}{2}$ oz wheatgerm

Blend all the ingredients for 30 seconds.

Note This is enough for 1 serving.

Mexican Chocolate

50g/2 oz plain chocolate
15g/$\frac{1}{2}$ oz instant coffee powder
4 drops vanilla essence
a pinch of ground cinnamon
450ml/$\frac{3}{4}$ pint hot milk

Cut the chocolate into squares and blend with the coffee powder, vanilla essence, cinnamon and milk until the chocolate has dissolved. Serve at once.

Note This is enough for 2 servings.

Peach Ginger

2 large ripe peaches
75g/3 oz caster sugar
$\frac{1}{2} \times 2.5$ml spoon/$\frac{1}{4}$ teaspoon ground ginger
a pinch of nutmeg
2×15ml spoons/2 tablespoons lemon juice
300ml/$\frac{1}{2}$ pint ginger beer

DECORATION
thin slices of orange

Skin the peaches and cut them into small pieces. Blend with the sugar, ginger, nutmeg and lemon juice for 30 seconds. With the motor running, pour in the ginger beer and then switch off the blender at once. Pour into glasses and decorate with thin slices of orange.

Note This is enough for 3 servings.

Tomato Juice

450g/1 lb fresh tomatoes
150ml/$\frac{1}{4}$ pint water
1 small onion
1×5ml spoon/1 teaspoon lemon juice
1×5ml spoon/1 teaspoon wine vinegar
$\frac{1}{2}$ bay leaf
a pinch of celery salt
1×5ml spoon/1 teaspoon sugar

Put all the ingredients into a saucepan and simmer for 10 minutes. Remove the bay leaf, and blend the remaining ingredients for 10 seconds. Strain into a jug and leave in a cold place for 2 hours. Stir well before serving and pour into small glasses.

Note This is enough for 6 servings.

Vegetable Health Drink

6 sprigs watercress
2 sprigs parsley
1 stick of celery
4 tomatoes
10cm/4 inch length cucumber
1 small onion
1×5ml spoon/1 teaspoon lemon juice
salt and pepper
300ml/$\frac{1}{2}$ pint water

Cut the watercress, parsley and celery in pieces. Skin the tomatoes and cut them in pieces, and cut the cucumber in pieces. Cut the onion in pieces. Blend all the vegetables with the lemon juice, seasonings and water until smooth. Serve very cold.

Note This is enough for 2 servings.

Yoghurt Shake

150ml/$\frac{1}{4}$ pint yoghurt
1 thin slice of lemon
15g/$\frac{1}{2}$ oz caster sugar
150ml/$\frac{1}{4}$ pint pineapple juice

Blend all the ingredients for 30 seconds.

Note This is enough for 2 servings.

Variations

Substitute buttermilk for the yoghurt. Some fresh fruit, such as pineapple or banana can also be added.

Index of Recipes

Anchovy Spread 50
Apple Butter 73
Apple Butterscotch Crumble 55
Apple Crunch 59
Apple Flummery 60
Apple Popovers 59
Apple Sauce 36
Apple Snow 62
Apple and Walnut Salad 34
Apple and Walnut Stuffing 43
Apricot Pork with Apple Sauce 28
Apricot Whip 60
Aubergine Dip 51
Aurora Sauce 38
Avocado Dip 52
Avocado Dressing 40

Bacon Soup with Sausage Dumplings 22
Bacon Stuffing 43
Baked Cheesecake 63
Baked Coconut Pudding 58
Baked Stuffed Mackerel 32
Bakehouse Lamb 30
Bakewell Pudding 62
Banana Bread 66
Banana Flip 75
Barbecue Sauce 36
Basic Ice Cream 64
Basic Poultry Stuffing 45
Basic Soft Cheese Dip 52
Beef Broth 19
Beef Fritters 27
Beef Olives 27
Biscuit Tortoni 64
Blackcurrant Flummery 60
Bread Sauce with Onion 36
Brown Sauce 36
Butter Icing 68
Butterscotch Sauce 74

Celery and Apricot Stuffing 44
Celery Soup 13
Cheese Crumb Soufflé 34
Cheese Rarebit Spread 50
Cheese Sauce 40
Chestnut Soup 13
Chicken and Bacon Pâté 48
Chicken in Curry Sauce 25
Chicken and Ham Loaf 25
Chicken Liver and Cider Pâté 47
Chicken Liver Pâté 48
Chicken Mousse 25
Chicken and Pea Soup 22
Chicken Soup with Parsley Balls 20
Chicken Spread 50
Chicken Vol-au-vents 26
Chilled Avocado Soup 16
Chilled Beetroot Soup 16
Chilled Cucumber Soup 16
Chocolate Crumb Cake 66
Chocolate Fudge Sauce 74
Chocolate Sauce 74
Confectioner's Custard 70
Cottage Cheese Drop Scones 67
Country Carrot Soup 14
Coventry Tarts 67
Crab Chowder 24
Cranberry Apple Sauce 37
Cranberry Relish 71
Cream Cheese Icing 70
Cream of Onion Soup 15
Creamed Fish Soup 24
Curry Sauce 37
Custard Sauce 74

Date Chutney 71
Date Whip 62
Devil Dressing 42
Devilled Egg Dip 52
Devilled Ham 50
Drop Scones 68

Egg Nog 76
Egg Sauce 40

Fish Cakes 31
Fish Puffs 31
Flavoured Butters 37
Florentine Soup 15
French Fritters with Cherry Sauce 56
Fresh Fruit Shake for Slimmers 76
Fresh Pea Soup 18
Fruit Mousse 61
Fruit Pancakes 56

Garlic Butter 37
Giblet Stuffing 44
Gooseberry Chutney 72

Ham and Green Pea Soup 23
Hawaiian Punch 76
Herb and Lemon Stuffing 44
Hollandaise Sauce 38
Honey Butter 37
Honey Lemonade 76
Honeyed Almond Roast Chicken 26
Horseradish Cream Sauce 38
Horseradish Dip 54

Ice Cream Soda 78
Indonesian Sauce 38
Instant Banana Mousse 60

Jelly Chiffon Pie 63
Jelly Whip 62

Kipper Pâté 46

Leek and Potato Soup 16
Lemon Cordial 78
Lemon Crumb Pudding 58
Lemon Flummery 61
Lemon Sauce 75
Low-calorie Dressing 42

Maltaise Sauce 38
Maple Butter 37
Marmalade Cream 61
Mayonnaise 40
Meal-in-a-glass 78
Meat Paste 51
Mediterranean Salad 35
Mexican Chocolate 78
Mocha Fudge Icing 70
Morning Cake 66
Mousseline Sauce 38
Mushroom Soup 14

One-pot Soup 20
Onion Sauce 40

Parsley Butter 37
Parsley Sauce 40
Peach Ginger 79
Pear Chutney 72
Pennywise Lamb Roast 30
Pepper and Onion Pickle 73
Pickle Dip 54
Pineapple Stuffing 44
Plain Omelet 34
Plum Chutney 72
Pork and Cabbage Soup 23
Potato Pancakes 67
Prune Stuffing 45

Queen of Puddings 58
Quiche Lorraine 34

Raisin and Nut Stuffing 45
Raisin Pudding 58
Raspberry Foam 61
Raspberry Sauce 75
Raspberry Water Ice 64
Red Tomato Chutney 72
Rich Mushroom Sauce 39
Royal Icing 70
Rum Sauce 75

Sage and Onion Stuffing 44
Salad Cream 42
Salmon Mousse 32
Salmon Spread 51
Sardine Pâté 46
Scotch Broth 23
Seafood Pâté 46
Shrimp Sauce 40
Smoked Fish Pâté 47
Smoked Salmon Pâté 47
Soured Cream Dressing 42
Split Pea Soup 18
Stuffed Liver 28
Stuffed Whole Plaice 31
Sunshine Salad 35
Sweet Devil Sauce 39
Sweet Soufflés 55
Sweet and Sour Pork 28
Sweet and Sour Sauce 39

Taramasalata 51
Thick Oxtail Soup 19
Tomato Juice 79
Tomato Sauce 39
Tomato Soup 13
Turkey Terrine 48

Vegetable Health Drink 79
Vichyssoise 16
Vinaigrette Sauce 43

Walnut Loaf 67
Watercress Butter 37
Watercress Soup 19
White Sauce 40
Winter Chicken Salad 35

Yoghurt Salad Dressing 43
Yoghurt Shake 79